BC

A(ANS

ACCOMMODATING CHRISTIANS

An Exegetical Commentary on First Corinthians Ten

BY

SPIROS ZODHIATES, TH.D.

AMG
PUBLISHERS
Chattanooga, TN 37422

Accommodating Christians

An Exegetical Commentary on
First Corinthians Ten

ISBN 0-89957-459-9

Printed in the United States of America
02 01 00 99 98 97 –R– 7 6 5 4 3 2 1

To Rich Pardy, Ph.D.
whose valuable editorial assistance
has been greatly appreciated.

Contents

Preface

As we face life, it is good to stop and examine how God dealt with our forefathers.

The character of God is always the same, but He does not always act the same. He reveals Himself in a variety of ways, but always to show that He is sovereign, omniscient and omnipotent.

Jesus Christ is God who walked this earth as we now walk, and thus He can understand our dilemmas. However, the liberation he gives us from the slavery of sin is not freedom from testing. Although Israel was liberated from Egypt, her people spent forty years in the wilderness where God tested their faithfulness. We would do well to study those testings and learn from them in order that we may not make the same mistakes they did.

The lesson we will learn is that with every testing God has a way out (*ékbasis* [1545], exit). He never leads us into a trap with no way out. So verse 13 is the key verse of the first paragraph which comprises verses 1–13. The exit is not always in the same direction and location, but there is an exit, and it is up to us to find it.

In 1 Corinthians 9:14–27, Paul compares life to a race. In that passage he calls the exit a "prize" (*brabeíon* [1017]).

There is, however, a distinct understanding that we who are on the road to the promised land shall encounter temptations by demons or evil spirits. We must be aware that they are there to oppose and confuse us. Their purpose is to divert our attention from God who is present in the midst of the wilderness of our escape from slavery to freedom. The road of freedom has but one exit, and we must not stray from the road that leads to that exit. Rest stops are attractive and desirable, but they will delay us from reaching the goal.

The key advice of the second paragraph of verses 14 through 22 is found in verse 14, where we are admonished to "Flee from idolatry." Idolatry is serving demons.

There is a providential rest stop for those who are traveling in the wilderness to the exit, and that is the provision of the Lord's table. We cannot partake of both the Lord's table and the tables of demons.

As Christians, we are endowed with a God-sensitive conscience which helps us decide matters that deal with the non-essentials of the Christian faith. One of these things is whether or not we may eat meats sacrificed to idols. The question which needs to be answered is whether such actions are self-serving or edifying and contribute to the general good of all believers.

The key verse of the third paragraph of verses 23 through 33 is verse 33: "In like manner, I accommodate myself to all people in all things, not seeking my own advantage, but that of many, so that they may be saved" (a.t.).

The bottom line of all considerations by any Christian is threefold:

(1) to know that God does not change, as demonstrated by Jesus Christ, God manifest in the flesh (Heb. 13:8)—1 Corinthians 10:1–13

(2) that in matters of our eternal salvation we must flee from idolatry—1 Corinthians 10:14–22, and

(3) in matters of non-essentials to the Christian faith, we must not impose laws determined by our personal preference—1 Corinthians 10:23–33.

If we act selfishly in disregard to others, we become a hindrance to the salvation of those outside of Christ. Hence the title of the book "Accommodating Christians."

SPIROS ZODHIATES

An Overview of First Corinthians

Author: Paul the Apostle, author of thirteen other epistles to various individuals and congregations.

Date: About A.D. 55.

Recipients: The congregation Paul had established in Corinth.

Place: From Ephesus

Theme: Paul had received news about the Corinthian brethren from several sources (1 Cor. 1:11; 7:1; 16:17). The church was afflicted with many of the problems that face young churches and new converts. The Apostle, under the inspiration of the Holy Spirit, decided to write this urgent letter to admonish and instruct the church. Among other topics he discussed: the necessity of church discipline (5:1–13); divisions and disputes among Christians (1:10–16; 6:1–11); matters of conscience (8:1–13; 10:19–33); the support of preachers (9:1–27); abuses of the Lord's Supper (10:16–17, 21; 11:17–34); the misuse of spiritual gifts (12:1—14:40); and the importance of the resurrection of Jesus Christ (15:1–58).

An Outline of First Corinthians

In the days of the Apostle Paul, Corinth was the capital city of the Roman province of Achaia and the glory of Greece. Though its great ancient splendor had been destroyed by the Romans in 120 B.C., the city was rebuilt under Julius Caesar and restored to wealth and luxury under Augustus. Among all the cities of the world, however, it was most well known for its lewdness. The Apostle Paul lived in Corinth for eighteen months (Acts 18:11). After his departure, Paul went to Ephesus. During his three-year stay there, he heard reports of wickedness and division within the Corinthian church. In an effort to correct these evils, Paul wrote several letters to them, including the Epistle of First Corinthians.

1:1–9	The introductory remarks of Paul.
1:10–16	Paul condemns the divisions in the church and exhorts its members to unity.
1:17—2:16	Paul defends his ministry. He has preached the wisdom of Christ crucified. This wisdom is foolishness to the world, but is the glory of all those to whom the Spirit of God has revealed the truthfulness of it.
3:1–5	Paul declares that the simplicity of his teaching was due to the carnal state of the Corinthians, which state is clearly evidenced by their divisions.
3:6–23	Jesus Christ is the only foundation. Ministers are mere servants; the work is God's.
4:1–6	The duty of ministers is faithfulness.
4:6–21	Paul contrasts the arrogance and conceit of the false teachers to the humility and sacrifice of the apostles. Using his unique position as their spiritual father, Paul calls on the Corinthian believers to be discerning.
5:1–13	Flagrant, sexual immorality was being practiced by one of the members of the congregation. Paul reproves

1 Cor. 10:1 | *Where God's Providence Leads, It Also Provides*

But, brothers, I do not want you to ignore the fact that our fathers were all under the visible cloud and all passed through the sea . . . .

The Christian life is compared to a race to be run with the purpose of obtaining a prize. Paul gives clear principles to be followed in 1 Corinthians 9:24–27.

We should remember that Paul, the author of the Epistles to the Corinthians, is not writing about salvation, but about our faithfulness in using our God-given abilities to the end. The Christian life is not a competitive endeavor of one with another. What we do with the gifts and grace of God which have been bestowed upon us is what matters. At the very beginning of his First Epistle, Paul said to the Corinthians in chapter 1, verse 4, "I thank my God always on your behalf, for the grace of God which is given you by Jesus Christ." Each Christian believer is a believer simply because he was given the grace of God by faith and accepted it. "For by grace are you saved through faith; and that not of yourselves: it is the gift of God: not of works, lest any man should boast. For we are His workmanship, created in Christ Jesus unto good works, which God has before ordained that we should walk in them" (Eph. 2:8–10).

Each one of us is an individual human being, acted upon by the grace of God. When we receive the grace of God, we do not cease to be individuals with differences in character and abilities. We must never forget the basic declaration of Paul in 1 Corinthians 4:7: "For who makes you to differ from another, and what do you have that you did not receive?" (a.t.). In 1 Corinthians 1:5 we are told, "That in everything you are enriched by Him, in all utterance, and in all knowledge." As a result of this abounding grace of God, we must realize that we "come behind in no gift [*charísmati* {5486}]; waiting for the coming of our Lord Jesus Christ" (1 Cor. 1:7). Paul is eager for us to realize and utilize our gifts.

Charísmata are the results of grace. Paul compares the utilization of the results of grace in our Christian life to a race that is to be run (1 Cor. 9:24–27). The word *adókimos* (96), unapproved, translated "cast away" should be viewed in connection with the proper utilization of our gifts and the commensurate reward that awaits us as individual Christians (2 Cor. 5:10).

"But"

First Corinthians 10, a continuation of 1 Corinthians 9:24–27, has the particle *dé* (1161), "but," in the Textus Receptus and Majority Text. Other texts have the particle *gár* (1063), meaning "therefore." Both particles provide a connection between the illustration of the race in chapter 9 and the historical activity of God in leading the Israelites out of Egypt.

Note that the word *pántes*, the nominative plural masculine form of the adjective *pás* (3956), "all," is used five times in verses 1 to 4:

"all our fathers were under the cloud" (v. 1)

"all passed through the sea" (v. 1)

"all were baptized unto Moses in the cloud and in the sea" (see v. 2) "all did eat the same spiritual meat" (v. 3)

"all did drink the same spiritual drink" (v. 4).

The repeated usage of this word "all" means that God did not exclude arbitrarily any of the children of Israel from being liberated from the land of Egypt. Any Jews refusing to come out of Egypt made this choice on their own initiative, disobeying God's command to leave. Paul, speaking of God, says in 1 Timothy 4:10 that He "is the savior of all [*pántōn*, the genitive plural masculine form of the adjective *pás*] men, especially of those that believe." Peter elaborates on this truth in 2 Peter 3:9: "The Lord is not slack concerning His promise, as some men count slackness; but is long-suffering to us-ward, not willing that any should perish, but that all should come to repentance." Therefore, God could not have been responsible for any Jews not choosing to leave the slavery of Egypt, for that offer of liberation represented the grace of God.

Exodus 12:38 tells us that "a mixed multitude went up with them also." Others who were not Israelites and who felt led to follow God's command to leave Egypt were equally under His protection and care as they took their journey into the wilderness. Peter unequivocally declared when he preached to Cornelius and the Gentiles in Acts 10:34–36, "Of a truth I perceive that God is no respecter of persons: but in every nation he who fears Him, and works righteousness, is accepted with Him."

We are, therefore, assured that God does not arbitrarily exclude anyone from the opportunity of liberation through His grace.

God Desires That All Should Be Saved

God had showed special favor to the Jews as a race: "And He said [to Jacob], 'Your name shall be called no more Jacob, but Israel: for as a prince you have power with God and with men, and have prevailed' " (Gen. 32:28, cf. 35:10). This special favor of God, however, did not apply to individuals insofar as the salvation which Jesus Christ was going to bring to all people by grace. As Paul asks in Romans 3:1: "What advantage then has the Jew, or what profit is there in circumcision?" Paul did not consider all the Jews to be saved, but only those who believed, even as Abraham did. In Romans 9:3 Paul wrote, "For I could wish that myself were accursed from Christ for my brethren, my kinsmen according to the flesh." So there should be no misunderstanding by equating the escape from Egypt to salvation. Rather, this is an example of the way God deals with mankind, and it shows that the character of God includes a desire to draw all men to Himself.

"Brothers, I Do Not Want You to Ignore the Fact"

Let us not forget that Paul recognizes three kinds of people, as he tells us in 1 Corinthians 10:32, namely: the Jews, the Gentiles, and the church of God which consists of both Jews and Gentiles who believe on the Lord Jesus Christ. And so he reminds us, first of all, not to ignore history, but to remember how God dealt with the Jews first and a multitude of others as He intervened in their lives and liberated them from Egypt.

Thus Paul begins this verse by saying, "Therefore" (*dé* but, also, now, moreover, in the TR and MT; and *gár*, therefore, consequently, in the UBS and Nestle's Text). This means that there is a definite connection between Paul's illustration of a race and the prize at the end of the race in 1 Corinthians 9:24–27. God, indeed, liberated all the Jews from Egypt, but He followed them in their sojourn to see if they were well-pleasing in their behavior. Sad to say, the Lord found the majority unpleasing (v. 5).

Paul is using the history of Israel to set an example showing how he wants the believers in Jesus Christ who have been liberated from the slavery of sin to behave acceptably before God and at the end of the road to receive the prize. Thus he says, "I do not want you [*ou* {3756}, the absolute not; *thélō* {2309}, wish, desire] to ignore [*agnoeín*, the present active infinitive form of *agnoéō* {50}, to be willfully ignorant] the fact." Paul did not want the Corinthians to disregard the consequences of such neglect.

"I do not want you to ignore" or "to be ignorant of" are favorite expressions of the Apostle Paul. The following instances in the New Testament in which Paul uses such expressions show us what is most important in life and what it is that we cannot ignore.

One of the occurrences is in Romans 11:25: "For I would not, brethren, that you should be ignorant of this mystery, lest you should be wise in your own conceits; that blindness in part is happened to Israel, until the fullness of the Gentiles be come in." Paul tells us here that indeed it is a mystery why the most favored people in the world, the Jews, rejected Christ, and why the idolaters, the Gentiles, in far greater numbers, welcomed Him. However, he tells us that one day all Israel will be saved (Rom. 11:26). Paul does not want the believers to be mystified by the great number of Gentiles who have accepted Christ, and he also wants them to know how God is going to end human history and save Israel in due time. Thus, we are told not to be ignorant of the mystery regarding the reason that the Gentiles more readily came to Christ, whereas the favored race of God, Israel, was so unbelieving.

In 1 Corinthians 12:1 Paul says: "Now concerning spiritual gifts, brethren, I would not have you ignorant." Then he goes on to state that the Gentiles have been saved in spite of the fact that they had been idolaters following dumb idols (v. 2).

Paul also uses this expression in 2 Corinthians 1:8: "For we would not, brethren, have you ignorant of our trouble which came to us in Asia, that we were pressed out of measure, above strength, insomuch that we despaired even of life." Paul explains here that the favor of God in granting salvation does not exempt one from suffering, struggle, and even death, for salvation does not change the corruptibility of our body. Believers suffer and die, even as unbelievers do, but he wants us to realize that death, for the believer, is liberation, and not something to fear. Verse 10 says, "Who delivered us from so great a death, and does deliver: in whom we trust that He will yet deliver us." Three times he uses the verb "deliver" which is the translation of *rhúomai* (4506), to deliver by drawing unto rather than away from. For the Christian, death is not leaving behind that which is most precious, but going to be with Christ which is far better than any earthly life (Phil. 1:23).

The last time that this phrase occurs is in 1 Thessalonians 4:13: "But I would not have you to be ignorant, brethren, concerning them which are asleep, that you sorrow not, even as others which have no hope." There is a great difference between the death of a believer and a nonbeliever. A believer knows where he is going when he dies, but an unbeliever does not, and dreads death. The believer is looking forward to his reward, his prize (*brabeíon* [1017]) mentioned in 1 Corinthians 9:24, or crown (*stéphanos* [4735]) mentioned in 1 Corinthians 9:25.

"That Our Fathers Were All under the *Visible* Cloud"

The congregation in Corinth was a mixed congregation made up of Jews and Gentiles. The Lord Jesus speaks of the Jews as "**your** fathers," but never "**our** fathers," as the Apostle Paul did. In a sense, the Israelites were spiritual fathers not only to the Jews, but also to the Gentiles. Paul, in Galatians 6:16 calls the believers in Christ "the Israel of God." In Galatians 3:6, Paul says, "Even as Abraham believed God, and it was accounted to Him for righteousness." And in verse 14 he says, "That the blessing of Abraham might come on the Gentiles through Jesus Christ;

that we might receive the promise of the Spirit through faith." Therefore, Paul spoke on behalf of both the Jews and Gentiles in the church of Corinth as the fathers of Israel being the fathers of all. (See also Romans 4:1–5.)

The verb "were" in the phrase "our fathers were all under the *visible* cloud" is *ēsan*, the imperfect of *eimí* (1510), to be. This indicates that the children of Israel were under (*hupó* [5259]) the general divine providence of God consequent to their leaving Egypt and during their entire journey.

They "all" (*pántes*, the nominative plural masculine form of the adjective *pás*, everyone, constituting the totality) were under the cloud. There are two Greek nouns that are translated as "cloud." There is the neuter noun *néphos* (3509) found only in Hebrews 12:1, which means a shapeless mass covering the sky, metaphorically meaning a great multitude, a throng. This throng which has preceded us to heaven can be compared to a huge multitude of people watching a race and cheering the runners on. We are urged to throw aside anything that would hinder us and press on. We are not running the race alone. There is a heavenly throng watching that knows the prize that is awaiting us, and they eagerly want us to win it.

The other word, *nephélē* (3507), is a feminine noun, a diminutive form of *néphos* which means a small, visible, and shaped cloud. This is the word used in 1 Corinthians 10:1.

In Psalm 104:3, we find it stated that the clouds are God's chariot, and in Exodus 34:5, we read "And the Lord descended in the cloud, and stood with him [Moses] there and proclaimed the name of the Lord." In Numbers 11:25, we find that "the Lord came down in a cloud, and spoke unto him, and took of the spirit that was upon him, and gave it unto the seventy elders: and it came to pass, that, when the spirit rested upon them, they prophesied, and did not cease" (cf. Deut. 5:22). Our verse in 1 Corinthians 10:1 refers to the historical instance of Exodus 13:21 where we read, "And the Lord went before them by day in a pillar of a cloud, to lead them the way; and by night in a pillar of fire, to give them light; to go by day and night." It is to the same event that Psalm 78:14 refers: "In the daytime also He led them with a cloud, and all the night with a light of fire."

One of the great events during the life of Christ was the experience of transfiguration. The story in the three instances of the synoptic gospels is presented as having taken place in the midst of clouds. In Matthew 17:5, it is called "a bright cloud" (*phōteinē* [5460], visible to the eye and giving light, luminous; *nephélē*, cloud [cf. Mark 9:7; Luke 9:34, 35]). Out of the cloud a voice was heard, the voice of God, affirming that Jesus Christ was His beloved Son and that those present should heed Him.

In Acts 1:9, we find that the Lord Jesus ascended into heaven in a cloud: "And when He had spoken these things, while they beheld, He was taken up; and a cloud received Him out of their sight."

Paul informs us that the believers who will be on earth at the Lord's coming will be caught up in the clouds to meet Him in the air. Their bodies will be changed into the likeness of the incorruptible resurrection bodies of the saints who have already died (1 Cor. 15:52–54; 1 Thess. 4:13–18).

In Revelation 1:7, we read, "Behold, He comes with clouds; and every eye shall see Him, and they also which pierced Him: and all kindreds of the earth shall wail because of Him. Even so, amen." In Revelation 10:1, we find a mighty angel coming down from heaven arrayed with a cloud.

The experience of the Israelites being led by God (Ex. 13:21, 22; 14:19, 24; 40:38) is here recalled by the Apostle Paul to indicate the Lord's general divine providence for all of them. This he expresses by the phrase "were under the cloud [*nephélē*]." Psalm 105:39 says, "He spread a cloud for a covering;

and fire to give light in the night." The cloud was God's sign of His accompanying the children of Israel as long as they followed the leadership of Moses. The last words of our Lord to His disciples were, "I am with you always, even unto the consummation of the age. Amen" (Matt. 28:20, a.t.). So it was with Israel until they reached their destination. The providence of God was assured for all, as Deuteronomy 31:8 says: "He it is that does go before you; He will be with you, He will not fail you, neither forsake you: fear not, neither be dismayed." And the Apostle says in Hebrews 13:5: "Let your conversation be without covetousness; and be content with such things as you have: for He has said, 'I will never leave you, nor forsake you.' "

The cloud was entirely brought about by God, and there was nothing that the Israelites could do to assist Him in His providence.

The preposition that is used to express the providence of God for all is *hupó*, under, in the phrase "our fathers were all under the *visible* cloud." This touches upon the general providence of God which the Lord Jesus affirmed in Matthew 5:45: "for He makes His sun to rise on the evil and on the good, and sends rain on the just and on the unjust." Not all the Israelites who were liberated from Egypt were righteous people, but God did not discriminate in taking them out of Egypt. This providence of God was not due to the worthiness of the recipients. In Matthew 6:26 our Lord said, "Behold the fowls of the air: for they sow not, neither do they reap, nor gather into barns; yet your heavenly Father feeds them. Are you not much better than they?" And then, in verses 28 and 30, He says, "Consider the lilies of the field, how they grow; they toil not, neither do they spin. . . . Wherefore, if God so clothe the grass of the field, which today is, and tomorrow is cast into the oven, shall He not much more clothe you, O you of little faith?" Our Lord affirmed that there is a special providence in the fall of the sparrow (Matt. 10:29) and that even the very hairs of our heads are numbered (v. 30). Although God gives His general divine providence to all, He observes their conduct and the choices which they make in the enjoyment of that providence. Within the general providence there is the specific privilege of choice, as demonstrated in Matthew 7:13, "Enter you in at the straight gate: for wide is the gate, and broad is the way, that leads to destruction, and many there be which go in thereat"; "Not everyone that says unto Me, 'Lord, Lord,' shall enter into the kingdom of heaven; but he that does the will of My Father which is in heaven" (7:21). In His general providence, Jesus gave specific opportunities for choice when He said to His disciples, "If any man will come after Me, let him deny himself, and take up his cross, and follow Me. For whosoever will save his life shall lose it: and whosoever will lose his life for My sake shall find it" (Matt. 16:24, 25). And in Matthew 18:3 the Lord said, "Verily I say unto you, except you be converted, and become as little children, you shall not enter into the kingdom of heaven." So there is the general providence of God supplied for all, but there are also the choices that we as individuals make while we enjoy His providences.

God's providence is not shown through creation alone, but also through the sustaining of everything He has created. This is affirmed by the Apostle Paul in Colossians 1:17, "by Him all things consist [*sunéstēke*, the third person singular perfect active indicative of *sunístēmi* {4921}, to hold together or to stand together]." If the elements God created did not hold together in their proper places and proportions, there would be chaos. What keeps the earth and moon in their orbits, or what keeps the planets on their unerring paths? God has them all within His design and control, and they obey Him perfectly.

"And All Passed Through the Sea"

The next clause in our verse utilizes the preposition "through" (*diá* [1223]): "and all passed through the sea." This is in reference to the Red Sea which is about 1,400 miles long and 220 miles broad at its widest part. The miracle that happened when the Israelites faced the Red Sea and were pursued by the Egyptian hordes is related in Exodus 14:21–31. This historical event is referred to by Stephen in his memorable dialectic in Acts 7:36 before being stoned to death: "He [Moses] brought them out, after that he had shown wonders and signs in the land of Egypt, and in the Red Sea, and in the wilderness forty years."

Paul also reminded the Corinthians about the special intervention of God when He saved the Israelites as they passed through the Red Sea. He put them under the cloud and took them through the sea, not permitting them to drown in it, as they were pursued by the Egyptians. This was a special providence of God which, according to Hebrews 11:29, involved faith. "By faith they passed through the Red Sea as by dry land: which the Egyptians attempting to do were drowned."

> And Moses stretched out his hand over the sea; and the Lord caused the sea to go *back* by a strong east wind all that night, and made the sea dry *land,* and the waters were divided. And the children of Israel went into the midst of the sea upon the dry *ground:* and the waters were a wall unto them on their right hand, and on their left. And the Egyptians pursued, and went in after them to the midst of the sea, even all Pharoah's horses, his chariots, and his horsemen. And it came to pass, that in the morning watch the Lord looked unto the host of the Egyptians through the pillar of fire and of the cloud, and troubled the host of the Egyptians, and took off their chariot wheels, that they drove them heavily: so that the Egyptians said, "Let us flee from the face of Israel; for the Lord fights for them against the Egyptians." And the Lord said unto Moses, "Stretch out your hand over the sea, that the waters may come again upon the Egyptians, upon their chariots, and upon their horsemen." And Moses stretched forth his hand over the sea, and the

sea returned to his strength when the morning appeared; and the Egyptians fled against it; and the Lord overthrew the Egyptians in the midst of the sea. And the waters returned, and covered the chariots, and the horsemen, *and* all the host of Pharoah that came into the sea after them: there remained not so much as one of them. But the children of Israel walked upon dry *land* in the midst of the sea; and the waters were a wall unto them on their right hand, and on their left. Thus the Lord saved Israel that day out of the hand of the Egyptians; and Israel saw the Egyptians dead upon the seashore. And Israel saw that great work which the Lord did upon the Egyptians: and the people feared the Lord, and believed the Lord, and His servant Moses (Ex. 14:21–31).

Thus, the providence of God not only put the Israelites under the cloud, but helped them supernaturally to pass through the sea *(diélthon,* the third person plural aorist active indicative of *diérchomai* [1330], to go through). Where the providence of God led the Israelites, the same providence supernaturally helped them pass through while they were pursued by the Egyptians. The preposition *hupó,* under, is thus followed by the preposition *diá,* through, with God providing a way out when there seemed to be no natural way to save them.

There are lessons to learn from the two verbs that are used in the last phrases of our verse: "that all our fathers **were** under the *visible* cloud, and all **passed** through the sea." The first verb "were" is *ēsan,* the imperfect indicative of *eimí,* to be. It means that this event providentially came to be, indicating that they were brought there under the leadership of Moses, and that the benediction of God was manifested through the cloud that He directed to be formed over the place where they were. They were all benefiting under the providence of God, whether willingly or unwillingly, as is the case with all mankind. Without God's grace, everyone would be destroyed in a short time. In this connection, let us not forget the awesome declaration of Paul in Colossians 1:17 that "All things in Him are held together" (a.t.).

It is good for us to realize that we are what we are and where we are only by the providence of God.

The other verb we should note in the second phrase is the verb *diĕlthon*, they passed or they went through. This is the third person aorist active indicative of the deponent verb *diérchomai*. A deponent verb is one that ends in the suffix *omai* which is the form of the middle voice but is used as if in the active voice. It indicates passing through as a voluntary action, as we find in Hebrews 11:29 that the Israelites went through the sea. They believed Moses. This is why they were willing to entrust their lives to his command to enter the sea between the two mountainous walls of water on both sides. Not one would have entered had they not trusted in Moses' leadership. Hebrews 11:29 says, "By faith they passed [*diébēsan*, the third person plural second aorist active indicative of *diabaínō* {1224}, to go through, which occurs only in the active form] through the Red Sea as by dry land."

These two verbs indicate that the Israelites were found where the providence of God led them, and they exercised faith in the words of God's servant Moses. We bring out this distinction in the two verbs because of the importance of the prepositions *hupó*, under, and *diá*, through, and the prepositions we will encounter in verse 2, namely *eis* (1519), into, and *en* (1722), in.

LESSONS:

  1. There are things in the Christian life that we must not ignore:
     a. We must not ignore God's favor upon certain people, like Israel, and that this is a mystery that cannot be understood but must be accepted (Rom. 11:25).
     b. There is a general providence of God which is extended to both the just and the unjust, such as the sun and the rain by which everybody benefits, whether they deserve it or not (Matt. 5:45).

c. In spite of the fact that God has demonstrated a special grace upon special groups, the opportunity is extended to all, such as the mixed multitude who went out of Egypt with the Israelites.

d. We realize that in spite of life being full of tribulations, God delivers us unto Himself (*rhúomai*, to deliver by taking unto oneself; 2 Tim. 3:11).

2. The Israelites, having been found where God placed them, exercised faith in Moses and obeyed him, thrusting themselves into the sea, which loomed before them as certain destruction. Because of their faith, they were participants in a great miracle.

3. As we examine history, which in reality ought to be interpreted as "His story," we can see the general providence of God, in this instance demonstrated by the deliverance of the Jews from Egypt and leading them through the desert. However, at the same time He covered them with His cloud to guide them.

1 Cor. 10:2

An Experience of Identification

> *And they were all baptized into Moses in the cloud formation and in the sea,*

The word "all" was used twice in 1 Corinthians 10:1. It denoted the providence of God, for **all** were under the cloud formation. It also denoted the faith the Israelites exercised in Moses, their God-provided leader, for **all** passed safely through the sea. God's providence extends to the just and unjust alike.

"And They Were All Baptized into Moses"

Note that the word "all" *(pántes,* the nominative plural masculine form of the adjective *pás* [3956]) occurs here in verse 2 for the third time and is the subject of the sentence in the Greek.

The verb "baptized" in the Textus Receptus and the Majority Text is *ebaptísanto,* the third person plural aorist middle indicative of *baptízō* (907), to baptize. The middle voice should be translated "were all baptized." This is the reading also of the United Bible Society and the Nestle's Text. The active form of the verb is *baptízō,* to baptize, and takes a direct object. The middle and passive voice is *baptízomai* which means to allow oneself to be baptized or to be baptized by someone else. To translate *ebaptísanto* as "were baptized" is to put the verb in the passive voice, which, as such, would have been *ebaptísthēsan.* This is

15

the reading of some critical texts. The verb *baptízō* is a technical New Testament verb meaning to dip or immerse, and the element in which one is baptized is water, used with the preposition *en* (1722), in. John the Baptist, in Matthew 3:11 and John 1:26, 31, 33, speaks of baptizing in water (*en* [1722], in; *húdati*, the dative singular neuter form of *húdōr* [5204], water). The preposition *en* can be implied by the dative *húdati*, which is translated "in water" (Mark 1:8; Luke 3:16). The element of baptism, however, can also be the Holy Spirit. John the Baptist asserted that he was baptizing in water, whereas the Lord Jesus Christ was going to baptize those who believed on Him "in the Holy Spirit" (Matt. 3:11; Mark 1:8; Luke 3:16; John 1:33; Acts 1:5).

Although to baptize requires some type of element, we find that here in 1 Corinthians 10:2 neither the element of water nor the Holy Spirit is mentioned. What we have here, instead of an element of baptism, is a person, and that person is Moses: "And they were all baptized into Moses [*eis* {1519}, unto or into; *tón*, the accusative singular masculine form of the article *ho* {3588}, the; *Mōusēn*, the accusative form of *Mōusēs* {3475}, Moses]." Moses was the man of God under whose leadership the Israelites were liberated from Egypt and were led into the wilderness. Moses was neither water nor the Holy Spirit. Thus in order to find out the meaning of this phrase, we must examine the verb *ebaptísanto*. We have seen already that this is the middle voice which should be translated "they allowed themselves to be baptized." By following Moses, they identified themselves with his purposes in sincere obedience to him. If it were not for the leadership of Moses, they would not have left Egypt and would not be in the wilderness experiencing the providence of God. When the Israelites were baptized into Moses, they accepted the covering of the cloud and followed it through the sea. God had separated the sea and held it back as though by two walls of water which enabled them to go through without even getting their feet wet. Both the cloud and the sea involved vapor and water. This is a simile of water baptism.

As the Israelites, by allowing themselves to be baptized into Moses, identified themselves with the faith and purposes of that great Old Testament leader, so the term "to be baptized into Christ" has a symbolic meaning to believers of being identified with Christ through faith. The expression "to be baptized into Christ" occurs in Romans 6:3 which says, "Or do you ignore [*agnoeíte*, the second person plural present active indicative of *agnoéō* {50}, to ignore or disregard the knowledge] that as many of us as were baptized into Christ Jesus were baptized into His death?" (a.t.). *Agnoéō* is the same verb with which Paul begins this chapter of 1 Corinthians 10 by saying, "But, brothers, I do not want you to ignore. . . ." Being dipped under water during baptism symbolizes our burial together with Christ. As Romans 6:4 explains, "Therefore we are buried with Him by baptism into death: that like as Christ was raised up from the dead by the glory of the Father, even so we also should walk in newness of life." If it were not for the spiritual symbolism of baptism, it would be an empty ritual.

Galatians 3:27 also has the expression "baptized into Christ": "For as many of you as have been baptized into Christ have put on Christ." Water baptism, therefore, is the simile of our old nature or old man being buried together with Christ that the body of sin might be destroyed, and that henceforth we should not serve sin anymore. Therefore, baptism symbolizes our confession of faith and our dying with Christ so that we can live in the victory of His resurrection (Rom. 6:6–14).

The phrase "baptized into Christ" has the same meaning as the expression to baptize "in the name of the Father and of the Son and of the Holy Spirit" as we find in Matthew 28:19.

The name of someone is a summary of all that he is and all that person stands for (Acts 8:16; 19:5; 1 Cor. 1:13, 15). When a woman marries a man, she takes her husband's name, thus identifying herself with him. In being baptized in the name of the Father and the Son and the Holy Spirit, the believer identifies himself as a member of the family of God.

"In the Cloud Formation and in the Sea"

Two additional prepositions are used in this verse other than *hupó* (5259), under, in the phrase "under the cloud," and the preposition *diá* (1223), through, in the phrase "through the sea" of verse 1. Now we have the preposition *eis* (1519), unto or into, expressive of motion in following the leadership of Moses. The fourth preposition is *en*, in, which expresses position. When the children of Israel followed the leadership of Moses unto or into (*eis*) Moses, they were said to be baptized into Moses. We might note that even though they were in the midst of a raging sea with the water as high as walls around them (it must have been a most frightening experience), yet they were exactly where God had led them and were miraculously protected by Him. Being in the middle of difficult places does not necessarily mean we are out of God's will. It may be the very center of His will.

LESSONS:

1. Baptism into Moses meant identification with him and his leadership as he delivered the children of Israel from Egypt.
2. Christian baptism expresses identification in Christ just as baptism into water envelops a person completely within that element.
3. Although baptism is not referred to in 1 Corinthians 10:2, the verb is used because it so well identifies the Israelites with Moses.
4. Water baptism is consequent and subsequent to identification with the death and resurrection of Jesus or the baptism by the Holy Spirit.
5. Sometimes in following Christ, we find ourselves in the middle of troublesome situations. God may allow this and use it for His glory.

1 Cor. 10:3

A Physical Event With Spiritual Meaning

And all ate the same spiritual food,

God's providence was shown to Israel by providing a visible cloud to guide them and by dividing the Red Sea for them to pass through. Thus the Israelites did not fall victim to the pursuing Egyptians.

"And All Ate"

In this verse we have the provision of God for the Israelites and the multitude with them while they were in the desert.

The "all" (*pántes*, the nominative plural masculine form of the adjective *pás* [3956]) is mentioned for the fourth time in this chapter, indicating God's nondiscriminating general providence. The main emphasis in this verse is not that God provided food from heaven, as described in Exodus 16:4–30, but that it was all identical (*tó*, "the," the accusative singular neuter form of the personal pronoun *ho* [3588] followed by *autó*, "same," the accusative singular neuter form of the personal pronoun *autós* [846], same, identical).

"The Same Spiritual Food"

When God created man, He placed him in a garden, not in the wilderness. The Garden of Eden had a splendid variety of trees which provided food for man to eat. God tested man's obedience when He asked him not to eat of a certain tree. Man, however, disobeyed God and ate of the one and only tree that was forbidden him. He reaped the consequences which had been foretold by God (Gen. 1:28–31; 2:9, 17; 3:2, 6). Man was given the opportunity to produce and eat a variety of food, but he wanted the one food that was forbidden. The trouble with man was spiritual, for he was dissatisfied with God's abundant provision. He was greedy and wanted more.

God favored Israel and acted to liberate them from Egypt, calling Moses to be their spokesman and leader. On this occasion, man was not able to cultivate the desert to produce food, so God made supernatural provision for his needs. Paul, in writing to the Corinthians, says, "And they all ate the same spiritual food." However, it was physical food, the bread from heaven (Ps. 105:40) which is also called the "corn of heaven" (Ps. 78:24). The same food was provided for Jews and the non-Jews alike, and there was no variety in the food that God provided. It was manna and quails (Ex. 16:4–30). That was their material food, and God gave them instructions regarding the partaking of it.

But why is Paul calling the food which was miraculously provided for the children of Israel in the desert "spiritual" (*pneumatikón*, the accusative singular neuter form of the adjective *pneumatikós* [4152])? The adjective "spiritual" here does not negate the physical nature of the food. The word *pneumatikón* pertained to the natural food miraculously provided by the Spirit of God. In Nehemiah 9:19, 20 we read these words:

> Yet You in Your manifold mercies forsook them not in the wilderness: the pillar of the cloud departed not from them by day, to lead them in the way; neither the pillar of fire by night, to show them light, and the way wherein they should go. You gave also Your good spirit to

instruct them, and did not withhold your manna from their mouth, and gave them water for their thirst.

As one reads the story of the provision of the food and the water by God in the desert, it becomes clear that God acted directly, not indirectly, in providing man's need.

We should pay special attention to the phrase, "You gave also Your good spirit to instruct them." God, in giving not only abundance but also variety in the Garden of Eden, gave man the opportunity to use the spirit that He had implanted in him to thank God and to acknowledge that all good things come from Him. And in the desert, when He acted supernaturally by providing food from heaven without man's cooperation, it would be expected that the spirit of man would acknowledge an even greater provision. The food was the same for all, and it was adequate for all, but man, who did not appreciate variety, originally did not appreciate adequacy either.

What Is "Spiritual Food"?

When the Lord Jesus was tempted by Satan, he said to Him, "If You are the Son of God, command that these stones be made bread" (Matt. 4:3). The Lord's answer was related to His provision of bread in the wilderness for the Israelites when He quoted from Deuteronomy 8:3, "And He humbled you, and suffered you to hunger, and fed you with manna, which you did not know, neither did your fathers know; that He might make you know that man does not live by bread only, but by every word that proceeds out of the mouth of the Lord does man live." God is Spirit, Jesus said to the Samaritan woman (John 4:24). Man is the only creature in whom God placed His Spirit so that when he eats material food, his spirit should be activated to thank God and acknowledge His provision in abundance and in sufficiency. That is why, we believe, Paul called the food which the Israelites ate in the desert "spiritual."

In 1 Corinthians 15:44, in which Paul discusses the body that we shall be given at the resurrection of the dead, he calls it a "spiritual body" as contrasted to the natural body which we now possess. The word "natural" is a translation of *psuchikós* (5591) which relates the body to the soul (*psuchḗ* [5590]) which man has in common with animals and other living creatures. Only in man did God put His Spirit so that as man enjoys material food, he might thankfully exercise the faculty of the Spirit in recognizing that material blessings come from God.

In the sixth chapter of John, after the Lord fed more than five thousand people with the multiplied loaves of bread and fishes, He gave His marvelous teaching, revealing Himself as the bread of life (John 6:35). This discourse of our Lord ought to be studied in conjunction with Paul's message in 1 Corinthians 10:3, 4. When man fell, he lost his relationship with God, but Jesus Christ came to bridge that gap. The Israelites ate the heavenly manna, but failed in their spirits to recognize God as the provider. This would be remedied with the coming of the Lord Jesus Christ who said, "I am the bread of life: he who comes to Me shall never hunger; and he who believes on Me shall never thirst" (John 6:35). He is our spiritual bread of which we need to partake by believing on Him.

The Israelites did not receive spiritual life merely by eating the physical manna that God had provided. The Lord, in John 6:63, says, "It is the Spirit that gives life; the flesh profits nothing: the words that I speak unto you, they are spirit, and they are life" (a.t.). This is why the categorical answer of our Lord to Satan was that "Man shall not live by bread alone, but by every word that proceeds out of the mouth of God" (Matt. 4:3).

Jesus came down from heaven just as the manna was sent down from heaven. He became the spiritual food that fallen man needs so that his spirit can be reconciled to God. The Lord Jesus in John 6:38 said, "I came down from heaven." The Jews who heard Him speak these words objected by saying that they knew that He was the son of Joseph (vv. 41, 42). They did not believe in the virgin birth of Christ, and they did not acknowledge His divine origin. This gave occasion for the Lord to answer and to proclaim the eternal words in verses 46–51:

> Not that any man has seen the Father, save He which is of God, He has seen the Father. Verily, verily, I say unto you, he that believes on Me has everlasting life. I am that bread of life. Your fathers did eat manna in the wilderness and are dead. This is the bread which comes down from heaven, that a man may eat thereof, and not die. I am the living bread which came down from heaven: if any man eat of this bread, he shall live forever: and the bread that I will give is My flesh, which I will give for the life of the world.

The Lord Jesus was, indeed, confirming that the purpose of His incarnation was to become the bread of life which gives eternal life to those who believe.

Paul speaks of the food that came from heaven in an allegorical sense as "spiritual," that is, pertaining to the spirit, but the verb he uses is "they ate" (*éphagon*, the third person plural second aorist active indicative of *esthíō* [2068], to eat, consume food, spoken both of men and animals). Undoubtedly this spiritual food referred to the food which God bestowed upon the Israelites directly from heaven, as the Greek word would indicate. When they ate this food, however, they accepted it as being only physical bread. They did not consider what it represented— the goodness and the providence of God. The Apostle Paul implies, however, that both the food and the water should have been received thankfully as spiritual gifts from God. In John 6:1–14 the Lord performed the miracle of feeding thousands by multiplying bread and fish. Let no man think that this was not real bread and real fish. Yet, after that miracle, the people referred

to the manna that the Jewish forefathers ate (*éphagon*) in the
desert (John 6:31). In verse 32, Jesus calls it the "bread from
heaven" which Moses had given them. He then added, "But My
Father gives you the true bread from heaven." The word "true"
is translated from *alēthinón* (228), real, genuine. Jesus appeared
on earth by becoming man so that He could die for humanity,
but before His incarnation He was eternally with the Father
(John 1:18). Speaking of His descent from heaven, Jesus called
Himself "the bread of life" (John 6:35). When He spoke these
words, the Lord Jesus had not yet sacrificed Himself on the cross,
nevertheless He said to those that heard Him, "I am the bread
of life: he that cometh to Me shall never hunger; and he that be-
lieveth in Me shall never thirst." He equated faith with partaking of His body. Therefore, eating the bread of life means
believing on Christ. The same apostle who refers to the manna
as having descended from heaven, also tells us in Ephesians
2:8, "For by grace are you saved through faith; and that not of
yourselves: it is the gift of God." The descent of Jesus Christ
through His incarnation, His death on the cross, and His resurrection were considered so important by Him that one of
the last acts of His life was to institute a memorial feast so that
His coming into the world and dying for it might be perpetu-
ally commemorated (Matt. 26:26–30; Mark 14:22–26; Luke
22:14–20; 1 Cor. 11:23–25). The Lord took bread and the fruit
of the vine and gave it to His disciples to eat and drink. Although He called it His body and blood, He told them to eat
and drink of it. He literally meant that His sacrifice on the
cross was to be accepted as an act of grace and was to be believed.
He was not telling His disciples to literally eat His body and
drink His blood. Paul explains this act by saying, "And when He
had given thanks, He broke it, and said, 'Take, eat: this is My
body, which is broken for you: this do in remembrance of Me'"
(1 Cor. 11:24).

In the same manner, the children of Israel should have understood that, as they partook of the manna from heaven, it was a spiritual experience, for it was provided in a miraculous way by God Himself.

LESSONS:

1. God not only stresses His protection, guidance, and preservation of the children of Israel in the wilderness, but also His sufficiency of provision. This is demonstrated by the word "all" used for the fourth time in verses 1 to 3.
2. God provides not only for those who please Him, but also for the unrighteous as well. His sun and His rain benefit all. Likewise His cloud and guidance to go through the Red Sea were for the good of all the multitude, not just the righteous ones.
3. There are those, however, who, looking beyond physical provision for their needs, discern the spiritual hand of God, and in partaking of their physical food, they see God also as the provider of their spiritual needs. These are those with whom God is well-pleased.
4. As the children of Israel experienced the descent of their food from heaven, so Christ speaks of Himself as having descended from heaven and being the "bread of life." This "bread" ought not to be thought of only as the physical body of Jesus Christ, but as the preexistent Christ, the Son of God, who has always been with the Father, on whom we are called to believe and to be saved (John 6:35, 46, 48–51).

| 1 Cor. 10:4 | *The Water of Moses and the Living Water of Christ* |

And they all drank the same spiritual drink, for they were drinking of that spiritual rock following them, and this rock had been Christ.

The Lord provided the sojourning Israelites not only with food, but also with water. The historical record of this is found in Exodus 17:1–7 and Numbers 20:2–13.

"And They All Drank the Same Spiritual Drink"

The water the Israelites drank was physical water, and it was provided for all (*pántes*, the nominative plural masculine adjectival form of *pás* [3956], all, an adjective used for the fifth time in these four verses). The Apostle Paul calls this water *póma* (4188), drink, from the verb *pínō* (4095), to drink. However, he calls this, as also the food in the previous verse, "spiritual" (*pneumatiktón*, the accusative of *pneumatikós* [4152], spiritual). By calling the food and water "spiritual," he was denoting its source who was Christ, who in His eternal existence is Spirit and who became flesh so that He could dwell among us. To show that Paul is speaking of real water, he uses the aorist form *épion* (they drank) of the verb *pínō* (to drink). The Israelites in the desert drank water provided supernaturally by God, a provision for which they should have been thankful and should have recognized as being a miraculous gift of God. Note that the verb translated "ate" is also in the aorist tense, *éphagon*, of verse 3.

"For They Were Drinking"

When we find the verb "drink" used again in the next clause, it is in the imperfect tense, *épinon*, and should be translated "they were drinking." This explains the use of the aorist "drank" (*épion*) in the previous sentence as referring to the provision of water by God during their whole journey through the desert. They did not drink only once, but continuously during their sojourn as they had need.

We are reminded here of the conversation which the Lord Jesus had with the Samaritan woman as told in the fourth chapter of John. He asked her for water to drink (v. 7). When Christ told her that He could give her a gift from God which would be water different than the physical water contained in the well, He identified it as "living water" (v. 10). Furthermore, when He told her that whoever drinks of this living water would never thirst again and that it would be in that person a well of water springing up into everlasting life (v. 14), the Samaritan woman greatly desired it. As Jesus sought physical water to drink, He offered her living water which would enable her not to thirst again. This living water was equivalent to the eternal life which Jesus came to give to those who believe on Him.

"Of That Spiritual Rock Following Them"

When Paul speaks of the spiritual water, he refers to it as having come out of a rock, for the water that Moses gave the Israelites to drink did indeed come out of a rock. Moses smote the rock, and life-giving water came from it, enough to satisfy all who were thirsty. Jesus Christ was smitten of God for our iniquities (Is. 53:4, 5), and from this Rock comes our spiritual life, the only Water that can satisfy all who are spiritually thirsty. "Let him that is thirsty come" (Rev. 22:17).

"Rock" in Greek is *pétra* (4073), the feminine of *pétros* (4074). This is the same word that the Lord used to describe Peter: "You are Peter [*Pétros*], and upon this rock [*pétra*] I will build my church" (Matt. 16:18).

Before the word "rock" in our verse, Paul uses the participle *akolouthoúsēs*. This participle is the genitive singular feminine present active of *akolouthéō* (190), to follow, to accompany. The phrase would then translate, "For they were drinking of the spiritual rock following [or accompanying] them." Although there are two historic instances of the provision of water (Ex. 17:1–7; Num. 20:2–13), this spiritual water and spiritual rock were following the Israelites every step of the way.

"And This Rock Had Been Christ"

Paul does not hesitate to identify this rock as Christ. He says, "And this rock [meaning that particular rock] had been Christ." This declaration clearly shows that Christ was the One leading the Israelites through the wilderness and providing the indispensable water for them to drink. Observe that the Apostle Paul does not say Jesus, but Christ. Christ is His eternal name which relates Him to all history, not only to those who lived during His incarnation.

Notice also that the verb used here, *ēn* (2258), had been, the third person singular imperfect indicative form of the verb *eimí* (1510), to be, is the same verb that is used in John 1:1 (3 times), 2, 4 (twice), 8–10 referring to the self-existence of Christ. In this context, when reference is made to created beings and to historical events, the verb *egéneto*, the third person singular second aorist middle deponent indicative of *gínomai* (1096), to become, is used as in John 1:3 (3 times), 6, 10, 14, 17. The Apostle Paul uses *ēn*, had been, to indicate the participation of Christ's identity with God the Father and God the Holy Spirit as He led the children of Israel through the wilderness providing all their needs. The Holy Trinity was the accompanying Rock with the necessary provision of water.

LESSONS:

1. The Israelites were accompanied by a spiritual Rock who provided their physical water and also the living water for everyone who would believe.
2. Christ was self-existent from the beginning, and He is permanently the spiritual satisfaction of everyone who drinks the water He gives.
3. Christ had always been the eternal Son in the bosom of the Father. He became man to reveal God to humanity.
4. Jesus is the incarnate Christ.

1 Cor. 10:5

Why Was God Displeased With Most of the Israelites?

> *But God was not pleased with the majority of them. For this reason they were scattered as corpses in the desert.*

When the children of Israel followed Moses out of Egypt, they had a misconception of freedom. They thought that they were going to be freed from further trials or tribulations as they lived a life of liberation from the Egyptians. But it proved to be otherwise. They wandered in a desert for forty years and experienced hardship in spite of being free from the Egyptians.

"But God Was Not Pleased With the Majority of Them"

"The majority" (*toís pleíosin* [4119]) stands in contrast to "all" (*pántes*, the nominative plural masculine of the adjective *pás* [3956], everyone) which is mentioned five times in the first four verses. God liberated and provided for them all, but in spite of His extraordinary divine providence, only two above the age of twenty, Joshua and Caleb, qualified to enter the land of Canaan (Num. 14:30–32). Let us not forget that the liberation of the children of Israel from Egypt and God's provision for all of them stands as a historical reference to the illustration that Paul gives in 1 Corinthians 9:24–27 in which he tells us about the prize that we must struggle to attain at the end of the race. Paul's illustration of the liberation of the Israelites from Egypt does not refer to salvation, but refers to God's provision and how little it is appreciated.

God was not at all pleased with most of the Israelites in their behavior in the wilderness. The negative "not" is the absolute *ou* (3756) when the Lord speaks of His displeasure, and the word for "pleased" is *eudókēsen*, the third person singular aorist active indicative of *eudokéō* (2106), to be well pleased, from *eú* (2095), well, and *dokéō* (1380), to think. God did not think well of the majority of the children of Israel. On the other hand, *eudókēsa* is the same verb that is used when God spoke from heaven about His Son Jesus saying, "This is My beloved Son in whom I am well pleased" (Matt. 3:17).

The Apostle Paul states it mildly indeed when he says that God was not at all pleased with most of the children of Israel whom He brought out of Egypt under the leadership of Moses. This we shall see as we examine the Greek words in depth. To truly get an idea of how God felt, we must go to Hebrews 3:16-19: "For some, however, having heard, provoked [or rebelled]." The Greek word is *parepíkranan*, the third person plural aorist active indicative of *parapikraínō* (3893), to provoke unto bitterness or anger, to exasperate. This verb is used only here and only in relation to the Israelites whom God liberated from Egypt and for whom He provided so sufficiently and miraculously. The word is derived from the preposition *pará* (3844), near, immediate vicinity or proximity, and the verb *pikraínō* (4087), to embitter. The noun "provocation" (*parapikrasmós* [3894], bitter provocation, exasperation) occurs both in Hebrews 3:8, 15 and in the Septuagint in Psalm 95:8 and refers to the sin of the Israelites in the wilderness during their forty years sojourn (Heb. 3:17); and the verb *parapikraínō*, to provoke unto bitterness or anger or exasperation, is used only in Hebrews 3:16. Both the noun and the verb are used in relation to the Israelites provoking God. And then Hebrews 3:16 continues with the statement, "For some, when they had heard, did provoke: howbeit not all that came out of Egypt by Moses." There were a few, such as Caleb and Joshua, who had faithful and grateful hearts.

Having stated that God became exasperated with the majority of the Israelites, the Apostle asks the question in verse 17, "But with whom was He grieved forty years?" The word translated "grieved" is *prosṓchthise*, the third person singular aorist active indicative of *prosochthízō* (4360), to be burdened, grieved, indignant, angry, derived from the preposition *prós* (4314), against, and *ochthízō* (n.f.), to be grieved, offended, indignant, which is from *áchthos* (n.f.) meaning burden, load, indignation. This verb is only used here and only in regard to the Israelites and their behavior in the desert. It means that their behavior was so repugnant to God in view of His evident providence that they became a burden to Him. He would have caused the death of every one of them, but in His mercy, He allowed two above the age of twenty out of the six hundred thousand, Joshua and Caleb, to enter the promised land (Num. 14:30–32).

"For This Reason They Were Scattered *as Corpses* in the Desert"

The Apostle continues in Hebrews 3:17: "*Was it* not with them that had sinned, whose carcasses fell in the wilderness?" Whereas here in 1 Corinthians 10:5 the verb translated "were scattered as corpses" (from the verb *katestrṓthēsan*, the third person plural aorist passive indicative of *katastrṓnnumi* [2693], to spread as on a bed) seems to lay the responsibility on God (Dan. 4:35), the responsibility is laid squarely upon the Israelites in Hebrews 3:17: "having sinned [*hamartḗsasin*, the aorist participle form of *hamartánō* {264}, to sin]." Their attitude and behavior is called "sin," and "the wages of sin is death" (Rom. 6:23). This is an irrevocable law of God, and it is especially applicable to those who have experienced the mercy of God in such a demonstrable way as the Israelites had.

God's anger and indignation are described by John in Revelation 6:16 as the "wrath of the Lamb." Whoever heard of a lamb being angry? And how can God be angry, since He is love? We mistake the consequence of sin as God's wrath. When we despise His sacrificial love for us for so long that it becomes utter rejection, then it becomes His wrath.

Jesus came the first time to become the *amnós* (286), the lamb to be sacrificed (John 1:29, 36; Acts 8:32; 1 Pet. 1:19). Every other time He is called *arníon* (721), a lamb which, if not accepted as the *amnós*, becomes the lion of the tribe of Judah (Rev. 5:6; 7:9, 17; 10:3). God's perfect love can be provoked to anger and wrath because He is not only love, but He is also justice (Acts 3:14; 7:52; 22:14; 2 Thess. 1:5; 2 Tim. 4:8; 1 John 2:1, 29). Deuteronomy 28:63 says: "And it shall come to pass, that as the Lord rejoiced over you to do you good, and to multiply you; so the Lord will rejoice over you to destroy you, and to bring you to naught; and you shall be plucked from off the land whither you go to possess it." God loves not because He is weak, but because He is strong. Romans 9:22, when fully understood, sets the qualities of God in their proper order. He is love (John 3:16; 1 John 4:8, 16). When responded to, love saves the sinner. It has power. But if, in spite all its manifestations, it is rejected, its power to save is turned to power to destroy. Now read Romans 9:22:

> But if [*ei* {1487}, the subjective 'if,' meaning suppose] God, willing [*thélō* {2309}], to show His wrath [to exercise His executive will] and to make His power [*tó dunatón* {1415}, His accomplishment] known, endured [*ēnegken,* the aorist active indicative of *phérō* {5342}, to bring] with much long-suffering [*makrothumía* {3115}, patience toward people] the vessels of wrath [*orgḗ* {3709}] fitted [*katērtisména,* the perfect mid-

dle participle of *katartízō* {2675}, to fit, prepare] to destruction [*apóleia* {684}, perdition, eternal ruin].

The messages of this verse are:

• God is a long-suffering God. He extends His love toward all. He stretches it and lengthens it (*makro-thumía*).

• Man can accept God's love and, through Christ's grace, He saves those who believe. It takes power to save a sinner and transform him radically.

• Individuals can become vessels (*skeúē* [4632]) of God's love.

• But those who stubbornly refuse to believe and receive God's love will be exposed to God's justice expressed in wrath which is His indignation toward love and salvation rejected.

• No one, however, can claim that God has prepared him for eternal destruction. He has fitted himself for it. The verb "fitted" is not passive, but middle. Morphologically, the middle and the passive are the same but the middle meaning must be attributed to it.

That the consequence of unbelief is going to be eternal destruction has been decided by God, but each individual decides to go to hell through his own refusal to believe, for God "will have all men to be saved and to come unto the knowledge of the truth" (1 Tim. 2:4), and as far as unbelievers are concerned, He is "not willing that any should perish, but that all should come to repentance" (2 Pet. 3:9). God prepared hell for the devil and his angels, and by refusing God's gift of salvation, a man personally chooses hell.

When God, therefore, punishes the unrepentant, He executes His indignation against evil. This explains why the verb for "grieve" in Hebrews 3:10, 17 is the unique verb *prosochthízō* which indicates that His punishment is a necessary burden upon Himself (*áchthos* [n.f.]) as a result of His justice. The more the Lord acts benevolently in man's life, the more responsible man is for his sin. The consequence of sin is inescapable.

LESSONS:

1. The character of God is love (1 John 4:8, 16).
2. He shows His general benevolence and providence toward all as His sun and rain falls upon each and everyone without discriminating between who deserves it and who does not, who is righteous and who is not.
3. When men, however, abuse the general providence of God and provoke Him, they provoke His love.
4. The third chapter of Hebrews ought to be read in conjunction with 1 Corinthians 10:5 to see how God's love was exasperated by man's misbehavior for forty years in the wilderness.
5. Psalm 95:10 ought to be read in conjunction with verse 5: "Forty years long was I grieved with this generation, and said, 'It is a people that do err in their heart, and they have not known My ways.'"
6. In spite of the fact that God is love, which He demonstrated by liberating the Israelites from Egypt, they provoked Him to bitterness (*parepíkranan* [3893]). His response to their behavior is called *parapikrasmos* (3894), from *pará* (3844), a preposition of close proximity, a reaction very close to human bitterness. It comes from *pikría* (4088), bitterness and the adjective *pikrós* (4089), bitter. We view bitterness as an evil pertaining to man. However, as an action of God, it cannot be evil bitterness. It is injured love, misunderstood justice.

1 Cor. 10:6 | *We Should Learn from the Behavior of the Israelites*

These things, therefore, became our examples so that we may not be desirous of bad things even as they desired . . . .

Verses 1 to 5 describe the history of God's liberation of the children of Israel from Egypt, His dealings with them during their forty-year sojourn in the wilderness, and their behavior. The study of history is important because it helps us to regulate the present and realize that the future is associated both with the past and with the present. History repeats itself, and he who learns from the past avoids the pitfalls of the present and lays the foundation of the future. "A page of history is worth a volume of logic," Oliver Wendell Holmes, Jr. declared.

"These Things, Therefore, Became Our Examples" •

"These things" translates from the neuter demonstrative pronoun *taúta*, which is the plural form of *hoútos* (3778). It refers to all the actions of God and how the Israelites responded to them. We must study carefully the teaching of Paul in Romans, chapters 9, 10, and 11 concerning Israel, and arrive at the same conclusion expressed in Romans 9:6, that ". . . they *are* not all Israel which are of Israel." We must also come to the same conclusion as he does in the seventh verse, "Neither, because they are the seed of Abraham, *are they* all children." In Romans 11:2, we find that God has not set Himself against Israel. He assures us in Romans 11:25 that the blindness of Israel and their obduracy is only until the fullness of the Gentiles is realized. It is then that all Israel shall be saved (Rom. 11:26).

In Romans 9 to 11 the prophecy concerning Israel is explained. Paul calls it *túpoi* which is translated "examples." The noun *túpos* (5179) is actually the visible mark, impression, or print caused by striking (*túptō* [5180]). Figuratively, the word acquires a moral sense indicating that we can learn from what others have done in order to regulate our own conduct. Observe that the word is given in the plural (*túpoi*, examples) and not in the singular (*túpos*, example). Paul has referred to the example of God's faithfulness to Israel, first in liberating them from Egypt, and then in providing for them during the forty years of their sojourn. He wants to remind us of the faithfulness of God and of His sufficient provision for our needs. At the same time, he wants to point out the examples of their ingratitude for God's miraculous provision and their grumbling against Him.

"So That We May Not Be Desirous of Bad Things Even as They Desired"

God used Israel's experiences in the wilderness as examples for us which is expressed by *eís tó* (*eís* [1519]; *tó* [3588]), in order that, so that. The relative "not" (*mḗ* [3361]) is used instead of the absolute "not" (*ou* [3756]) because of our fallen nature. The grace of God can give us victory over temptations, but Satan will never leave us without them.

What is it that we should not desire? The adjective *epithumētás* which is the plural accusative form of *epithumētḗs* (1938) is found only here. The verb *epithuméō* (1937), to have the affections directed toward something, to desire or long after, can be used in a good sense (Matt. 13:17; Luke 22:15; 1 Tim. 3:1; Heb. 6:11; 1 Pet. 1:12) and as a result of physical needs (Luke

15:16; 16:21), or in a bad sense of coveting and lusting after something (Matt. 5:28; Rom. 7:7; 13:9). It is evident that here in 1 Corinthians 10:6 the verb *epethúmēsan*, the aorist form of *epithuméō,* is used to refer to the sinful desire of the Israelites to eat flesh, as recorded in Numbers 11, and to reject the food which God miraculously supplied to satisfy their hunger. This sinful desire of the Israelites is characterized by the Apostle Paul as "bad" because they complained against the Lord (Num. 11:1). This is not called "evil" by the Apostle Paul, simply "bad." The Greek word is *kakón* (2556), bad, not *ponērón* (4190), evil or malevolent. Wanting a variety of food was not harmful or wicked, but the dissatisfaction of the Israelites with what God had given them was bad, for they complained against Him and His servant Moses.

LESSONS:

1. As we examine history, we must learn from it.
2. We must discern the providence and provision of God, and we must thank Him for it.
3. We must study the different events in our lives to learn from them.
4. To seek to better our conditions of life is not bad unless we complain against God for the things He has given us already.

1 Cor. 10:7

Idolatry Leads to Sensuality

Neither become idolaters even as some of them did, as indeed it has been written, "The people sat down to eat and to drink, and rose up to play."

In verse 6, after describing the faithfulness of God and the ingratitude of the Israelites, Paul tells the Corinthians that these events ought to be examples of what the proper attitude should be toward God's provision and providence. In verses 7 to 10, he delineates the principles of conduct that should characterize the Corinthian Christians.

"Neither Become Idolaters Even as Some of Them *Did*"

This verse begins with the negative conjunction *mēdé* (3366) meaning neither, not even, and is derived from the relative negative *mḗ* (3361), not, and *dé* (1161), but, and. Verses 8, 9, and 10 also begin with the word *mēdé*.

The Corinthians lived in a predominantly idolatrous environment. Today, as one visits ancient Corinth, two sights are conspicuous. One is the huge Temple of Aphrodite high on a hill overlooking ancient Corinth which is called Acrocorinth. In this temple a thousand prostitutes served as priestesses. The second impressive sight is the remaining columns of a beautiful temple dedicated to Apollo, the god of light, health and healing, music, poetry, prophecy, etc. Only in 1 Corinthians 8:10 is an idol temple (*eidōleíon* [1493]) mentioned. Of the eleven times that word "idol" (*eídōlon* [1497]) occurs, it is found five of those times in Paul's Corinthian epistles (1 Cor. 8:4, 7; 10:19; 12:2; 2 Cor. 6:16). Of the ten times that the phrase "meat sacrificed to idols" (*eidōlóthuton*) [1494]) occurs in the New Testament, six of those times it is found in 1 Corinthians (8:1, 4, 7, 10; 10:19, 28). Of the seven times that the word "idolater" (*eidōlolátrēs* [1496]) occurs in the New Testament, it appears four of those times in 1 Corinthians (5:10, 11; 6:9; 10:7). In 1 Corinthians 10:14 Paul denounces idolatry and urges the Corinthians to flee from it.

The Corinthians lived in an idolatrous environment. Thus, it makes sense that Paul, having used the exodus of Israel from Egypt and their descent into idolatry as an example, commands them to not become idolaters. The word is *eidōlolátrēs*, (idolater), derived from *eídōlon*, idol, and *látris*, which is not found by itself in the New Testament, but which means a servant, a worshiper. It is derived from the noun *latreía* (2999), worship which includes service and service which includes worship. Therefore, *eidōlolátrēs* is one who bows the knee to an idol, as if it were God, and serves such an idol. Christ explained to the Samaritan woman that "God is spirit" (John 4:24), not something tangible on which we can lay our hands. The Ten Commandments which the Lord delivered to the Jews through Moses included a forbiddance of any tangible, visible representation of God.

The Only Visible Form of God

However, in order that God might speak to man understandably, He took upon Himself a visible form. There is a difference, however, between the concept of God as an idea in the mind of man and God as He really is. If God is only what is conceived by the human mind, he cannot be any greater than the mind that imagined His experience. There are two Greek words related to this concept which we would do well to examine. The first is the word *schḗma* (4976), figure, external form or shape, which occurs first in 1 Corinthians 7:31 translated as "fashion" in the sentence ". . . for the fashion of this world passes away." This means the world (*kósmos* [2889]) is so huge that in order to be meaningful to man it has to be reduced to a particular fashion which man can experience and comprehend. The shape man gives to the world passes away. It is not constant nor consistent. The second occurrence of *schḗma* is found in Philippians 2:8 and refers to the incarnation of God in Jesus Christ. The Spirit-guided pen of the Apostle Paul wrote: "And being found in fashion [*schḗmati*] as man." This refers to Jesus Christ who in His eternal existence had been *lógos* (3056), intelligence, thought (John 1:1). In John 1:14 we read that this ever existing *lógos* became (*egéneto*, the aorist middle deponent indicative of *gínomai* [1096], to become) of His own volition and power that which He was not before. He became "man" (*ánthrōpos* [444]). He became a human personality who could be communicated with and who could communicate. He did not become simply a statue or some such thing that did not have the element of life (John 1:4). Had God become a statue representing a lifeless material object, then Christianity could be considered as idolatry. But Paul states that Christ had the form (*morphḗ* [3444], *nature*) of God: "Who being [*hupárchōn*, the present participle of *hupárchō* {5225}, existing prior to the shape He now has) in the form [*morphḗ*] of God, thought it not robbery to be equal with God" (Phil. 2:6). Because Jesus Christ was always in the bosom of the Father (John 1:18), and because He was God (John 1:1c), He could become the virgin-born, miracle-working living person, who took upon Himself the shape (*schḗma*) of man and not of an inanimate statue. He came to reveal God in a language man could understand.

God became the unique man (*monogenḗs* [3439]; see John 1:14, 18; 3:16, 18; Heb. 11:17; 1 John 4:9) so that He could die and on the third day raise Himself from the dead, preaching His deity while He sojourned on earth as the God-Man (Matt. 16:21; 26:32; Mark 16:7). Jesus Christ was indeed the incarnation of God who came to tell us that God is a Trinity: God the Father, God the Son, and God the Holy Spirit. In 2 Corinthians 4:4, Paul tells us that Christ is the image (*eikṓn* [1504]) of God. In Colossians 1:15, speaking of Christ, Paul says, "Who is the image [*eikṓn*] of the **invisible** God, the firstborn of every creature." These verses tell us that God is not simply material, and that Jesus Christ became the visible image (*anḗr* [435], man) of God. First Corinthians 11:7 implies that it takes man, a living creature, to be the image of God and indeed the glory (*dóxa* [1391]) of God.

Paul, when visiting Athens, was disturbed and provoked by seeing the city full of idols (*kateídōlon* [2712]). In speaking with the Athenians, he intimated that idols are made with human hands (see Acts 17:24, 25), the products of man's imagination. But Jesus Christ was not a product of human design for He was conceived of the Holy Spirit (Luke 1:26–37). Speaking of the role of the Lord's virgin mother, Paul says in Galatians 4:4, "But when the fullness of the time was come, God sent forth His Son, made [*genómenon*, the aorist middle participle of *gínomai* {1096}, to become] of a woman." The mother of Jesus was not alone responsible for bringing Christ, who was the image and glory of God, into the world. Christ, as the God-Man, was not made by the coming together of a male and a female, as John 1:13 so eloquently proclaims: "Who [referring to the Word who is the subject of this total passage; see author's study in his exegetical commentary on John 1:1–18 entitled *"Was Christ God?"*] was born, **not of blood** [*haimátōn*, the genitive plural neuter of *haíma* {129}, blood] nor of the will [*thelḗmatos*, the genitive singular of *thélēma* {2307} which here, as in 1 Cor. 7:37 and Eph. 2:3, refers to human passion] of the flesh, nor of the passion of a husband [*andrós*, the genitive singular masculine of *anḗr* (435), meaning a male human being, which, in this instance, means husband and not man generically], but of God." God, the Holy Spirit, is the One who conceived Jesus Christ and chose the virgin Mary to give birth to Him. This is why Christ is never called an idol of God, but the image of God. He became the visible form of the invisible God.

The first commandment declared the uniqueness of God who is Spirit (Ex. 20:2; John 4:24). The second commandment was the prohibition against making any graven image, that is, an idol, to be worshiped (Ex. 20:3–5). An idol is anything that represents an imaginary deity. The Israelites said to Aaron as they waited for Moses to come down from Mount Sinai, "Up, make us gods, which shall go before us; as for this Moses, the man that brought us up out of the land of Egypt, we do not know what is become of him" (Ex. 32:1). And then, in verse 4, we read, "And he received them at their hand, and fashioned it with a graving tool, after he had made it a molten calf: and they said, 'These be your gods, O Israel, which brought you up out of the land of Egypt.'"

"As Indeed It Has Been Written, 'The People Sat Down to Eat and Drink'"

And then in Exodus 32:6 we read, "And they rose up early on the morrow and offered burnt offerings, and brought peace offerings; and the people sat down to eat and to drink, and rose up to play." The Lord certainly showed His displeasure by saying to Moses, "Go, get you down; for your people, which you brought out of the land of Egypt, have corrupted themselves: they have turned aside quickly out of the way which I commanded them: they have made them a molten calf, and have worshiped it, and have sacrificed thereunto, and said, 'These be your gods, O Israel, which have brought you up out of the land of Egypt'" (vv. 7, 8). Isaiah refers to this in Isaiah 2:8 when he says, "Their land also is full of idols; they worship the work of their own hands, that which their own fingers have made." In Isaiah 40:18–20, he continues: "To whom then will you liken God? or what likeness will you compare unto Him? The workman melts a graven image, and the goldsmith spreads it over with gold, and casts silver chains. He that is so impoverished that he has no oblation chooses a tree that will not rot; he seeks unto him a cunning workman to prepare a graven image, that shall not be moved" (cf. Is. 41:6, 7; 44:9–20).

Whatever, then, man makes with his hands as a representation of God and puts up as a god to be worshiped, is an idol. A Christian cannot be an idolater, a worshiper of a god made with hands. Unfortunately, Christendom with its statues and images made by hands as imaginary representations of God has become an idolatrous religion. As Israel was bearing the name of Israel but was not true Israel, so a person who bears the name of Christ and worships idols is not a true Christian.

"And They Rose Up to Play"

The verb *anéstēsan*, they rose (the third person plural aorist active indicative of *anistēmi* [450], to rise) stands in contrast to sitting down to eat and drink. One sits down to enjoy life by eating and drinking, but generally stands up to play.

But what is wrong with playing? The word "play" (*paízō* [3815]), occurs only here in the New Testament and is a quotation of Exodus 32:6. It repeats the story of the children of Israel making a golden calf at the foot of Mt. Sinai while Moses was on the mountain conversing with God (Ex. 32:1–6). We do not know what "to play" involved, but most probably it involved orgies of drunkenness which included fornication and sexual indulgence.

We conclude this from the fact that whenever the word "idolater" (*eidōlolátrēs* [1496]) is mentioned, it is in company with the word "fornicators" (*pórnos* [4205]) as in 1 Corinthians 5:10, 11; 6:9; Ephesians 5:5; Revelation 21:8; 22:15; and "idolatry" (*eidōlolatreía* [1495]) is in company with the noun "fornication" (*porneía*) as in Galatians 5:19, 20; Colossians 3:5 and also 1 Peter 4:3 where "lasciviousness" (*asélgeia* [766], insatiable desire for fleshly pleasure) is used instead of the word "fornication."

There are two evils from which Paul urges the Corinthian Christians to flee—fornication (1 Cor. 6:18) and idolatry (1 Cor. 10:14) which leads to fornication because idols are not deities. They are made by human hands while God is spirit (John 4:14) and can be genuinely worshiped spiritually (John 4:23). Debauchery is the product of idolatry.

LESSONS:

1. Idolatry is an abomination to the Lord. It reduces the true God who is spirit to things made by hand.
2. In Corinth, idolatry was such a danger to the Christians that Paul advised them to flee from it.
3. Idolatry is always connected with licentiousness and moral degeneracy.
4. Idolatry does not permit anyone to win the race of life, because it is not a climate of moral self-control (1 Cor. 9:25).
5. Christians are admonished to overcome the passions of the flesh (Gal. 5:16, 19–21), for they are people who are indwelt by the Spirit of God and, consequently, crucified in the flesh. This stands in contrast to the orgies that accompanied idolatry, the philosophy of which is "Let us eat, drink, and be merry." Play here means pleasure or fun that has no restraint.

| 1 Cor. 10:8 | *Fornication Is a Sin That Incurs the Wrath of God* |

> *Neither let us engage in fornication, even as some of them committed fornication and twenty-three thousand fell in one day.*

Paul connects the practice of fornication with idolatry. In 1 Corinthians 6:18 he gives the explicit command, "Flee fornication." In 1 Corinthians 10:14 he says, "Flee from idolatry." One of the idolatrous practices was fornication, for even the idol temples of Corinth had temple priestesses who were nothing more than prostitutes.

"Neither Let Us Engage in Fornication"

Paul now changes from the second person present imperative, "neither become [*gínesthe* {1096}] idolaters," of verse 7, to the first person plural present active subjunctive *porneúōmen* (4203) which we have translated, "Neither let us engage in fornication." This is a principle which Paul applied to himself and gave as advice to the believers whom he was addressing.

In Numbers 25:1 we read, "And Israel abode in Shittim [the last encampment of the Israelites on the east of the Jordan opposite Jericho], and the people began to commit whoredom with the daughters of Moab." Their idolatrous practices continued (v. 2), for sexual immorality usually accompanies idolatry

(1 Cor. 5:10, 11; 6:9; Gal. 5:19, 20; Eph. 5:5; Col. 3:5). When a man's god is no greater than his own imagination, degeneracy quickly sets in and evil multiplies.

"Even as Some of Them Committed Fornication and Twenty-Three Thousand Fell in One Day"

In 1 Corinthians 6:9, 10 Paul tells us that neither fornicators, idolaters, adulterers, effeminate, nor homosexuals will inherit the kingdom of God. This is quite a listing, and it is interesting to note, and a warning, that these sexual sins are mentioned in the same context as idolatry. Paul is stressing to the Corinthians how severely God dealt with those who committed fornication. He says, "And in one day fell [*épeson*, the third person plural second aorist active indicative of *píptō* {4098}, to fall] twenty-three thousand." He does not say that the Lord struck them dead for their sin, but simply that they fell, as if to say they reaped the consequence of their sin. This is a polite way of saying that the consequence of sin is God's punishment (Jude 5; Rev. 2:23).

An inconsistency seems to arise here between the figure given in the account in Numbers 25:9 and that of Paul in our verse. We can safely assume that the number who died was not exactly twenty-three thousand, but a generalization of somewhere between twenty-three thousand and twenty-four thousand, thus accounting for the two different figures.

LESSONS:

1. Idolatry should be avoided because it leads to sexual sins.
2. We are admonished to "Flee fornication," for "the wages of sin is death."
3. When left to his own imagination, mankind quickly degenerates.

| 1 Cor.
10:9 | *God Will Not Tolerate*
Man's Testing |

Neither let us engage in putting Christ to the test as some
of them tested Him, and they were destroyed by snakes.

Again, as in verse 8, Paul includes himself in his admonitions
to the Corinthians. The Old Testament incident to which Paul
alludes is recorded in Numbers 21:4–6:

> And they journeyed from Mount Hor by the way of the Red Sea,
> to compass the land of Edom: and the soul of the people was much dis-
> couraged because of the way. And the people spoke against God, and
> against Moses, "Wherefore have you brought us up out of Egypt to die
> in the wilderness? For there is no bread, neither is there any water;
> and our soul loathes this light bread." And the Lord sent fiery ser-
> pents among the people, and they bit the people; and much people of Is-
> rael died.

"Neither Let *Us* Engage in Putting Christ to the Test"

"Neither [*mēdé* {3366} as in vv. 7, 8] should we engage in putting
Christ to the test [*ekpeirázōmen*, the first person plural present
active subjunctive of *ekpeirázō* {1598} derived from the preposition *ek* {1537}, an intensive, and *peirázō* {3985}, to tempt]." The
compound verb found in this verse is found also in Matthew 4:7,
Luke 4:12; 10:25 and means try, prove, or test.

We have elected to translate this verb as "let *us* engage in putting . . . to the test." The basic verb *peirázō*, to try or prove, can be used in either a good or a bad sense. Here it is used in a bad sense indicating evil intent (Mark 8:11; 10:2; 12:15; Luke 11:16; 20:23; John 8:6). Men are said to prove or tempt God by doubting and distrusting His power and aid (Acts 5:9; 15:10; 1 Cor. 10:9; Heb. 3:9 quoted from Ps. 95:9; Sept.: Ex. 17:2; Is. 7:12). This is stressed by the preposition *ek* used as an intensive in *ekpeirázō*. Sinners are said to tempt God to the point of provocation, as did Satan (Matt. 4:7; Luke 4:12) and an unbelieving lawyer (Luke 10:25). Sapphira agreed with her husband, Ananias, to tempt the Spirit of God by lying and thinking that they could hide their deceit (Acts 5:9).

Satan tempted Jesus by taking Him to the pinnacle of the temple and challenging Him to throw Himself down, saying that if He was indeed the Son of God as He claimed, God would miraculously protect Him. The Lord answered Satan by quoting Deuteronomy 6:16: "You shall not tempt the Lord your God" (Matt. 4:6, 7). The Lord does not prove His deity by performing the signs that men demand of Him. He is not a man as we are and does not react to the whims of others. In Matthew 16:1, the Pharisees and Sadducees came to Jesus tempting Him and asking Him to show them a sign in proof of who He claimed to be. The Lord refused, not because He could not show them an additional sign, but because His predicted resurrection was going to be the final and most conclusive sign of His deity. Thus the Lord said, "A wicked and adulterous generation seeks after a sign; and there shall no sign be given unto it, but the sign of the Prophet Jonah [referring to Christ's resurrection]. And He left them, and departed." The Lord refused to perform additional miracles to satisfy the curiosity of those who challenged Him and refused to believe (Matt. 16:4).

It is interesting that the Apostle Paul, primarily referring to the incident recorded in Numbers 21:4–6, does not give the object of the testing as being God the Father, which was the case with the Israelites. Rather he says, "Neither should we engage in putting **Christ** to the test." This is an indirect affirmation of Jesus Christ being God, although not the same Person as the Father. We are reminded of the explicit declaration of John 1:1c: "And the Word [*Logos*] was God." It was precisely because of His claims to deity that Jesus was tempted on earth (cf. Luke 4:5–13; Col. 1:15).

"As Some of Them Tested Him"

In the Scriptures there is much evidence that not only did Satan test Jesus (Matt. 4:7; Luke 4:12) and unbelievers challenged Him (Luke 10:25), but also believers tested Him (Acts 5:9). Paul does not use the verb in the second person singular or plural imperative, but in the first person plural present subjunctive *ekpeirázōmen*. This includes himself and other believers, "Neither let **us**. . . ." The work of Moses in liberating Israel from Egypt and in leading them through the wilderness is a type of the work that Christ came to do on earth. John 3:14 refers to the incident in Numbers 21:4–6 by saying, "As Moses lifted up the serpent in the wilderness, even so must the Son of man be lifted up." He related this action of Moses to the work that Christ had come to do, "that whosoever believes in Him should not perish, but have everlasting life" (v. 15). In the wilderness, there were those who looked at the serpent on the pole, and they were saved. Thus also, when Christ was lifted up on the cross, there are those who looked to the cross and believed and were saved, but there were also those who did not and perished. In 1 Corinthians 10:7–10, the phrase "some of them" (*tinés*, the nominative plural masculine indefinite form of the pronoun *tis* [5100], someone) is used four times:

Verse 7: "Neither be you idolaters, as were **some of them** [*tinés*]; as it is written, " 'The people sat down to eat and drink and rose up to play.' "

Verse 8: "Neither let us commit fornication as **some of them** [*tinés*] committed, and fell in one day three and twenty thousand."

Verse 9: "Neither let us tempt Christ, as **some of them** [*tinés*] also tempted, and were destroyed of serpents."

Verse 10: "Neither murmur you, as **some of them** [*tinés*] also murmured, and were destroyed by the destroyer."

These were unbelievers who were Israelites, but not the true Israel of God (cf. Rom. 9:6). That some Israelites were not the true Israel of God is evidenced by the fact that they became idolaters (Ex. 32:1–8). First Corinthians 10:5 tells us that those against whom God was displeased were in the majority (*toís*, the dative plural masculine of the article *ho* [3588]; *pleíosin*, the dative plural masculine comparative form of the adjective *pleíon* [4119], more, majority).

The logical conclusion is that those who are following God, even like Aaron or Peter, can and do sometimes tempt Christ or put Him to the test. The Apostle Paul here is careful not to exclude himself by saying, "Let **us** not engage in putting Christ to the test." If the Apostle Paul included himself, how much more we should beware lest we fall? It behooves us, then, to know how we are likely to put Christ to the test, so that we may be forewarned.

How Do We Test Christ?

Let us consider the Israelites. How did they put God and Moses to the test?

They thought that their troubles would be finished the moment they were liberated from Egypt. In a similar manner, we who are believers sometimes fall into the same trap when we are redeemed by Jesus Christ from our sins and are saved. We think that our agenda of life is better than God's, and that it should be free from suffering and hardship. We must never forget the words of Christ in Matthew 11:28: "Come unto Me, all you that labor and are heavy laden, and I will give you rest." The word for "rest" here is *anápausin* (372) which means inward tranquility while one performs necessary labor which entails weariness. This word is in contrast to *katápausis* (2663) which means rest that comes from cessation of work and fatigue. The same Christ who spoke this verse concerning inner rest, tranquility, and peace, also said in John 16:33, "These things I have spoken unto you, that in Me you might have peace. In the world you shall have tribulation [*thlípsis* {2347}, affliction, pressure]: but be of good cheer; I have overcome the world." We, as believers, in actuality tempt our Lord when we claim that in addition to His inner peace He should give us exemption from the common sufferings of life which are the consequence of Adam's sin. When Satan tempted the first couple in the Garden of Eden, he put into their minds the desire to know both "good and **evil**." That desire was fulfilled, and mankind has suffered from evil ever since. "And He gave them their request; but sent leanness into their soul" (Ps. 106:15). How can we experience evil without suffering its consequences? This is an impossibility. As Job 5:7 says, "Man is born to trouble, as the sparks fly upward." The good news is that our complete redemption (*apolútrōsis* [629]), which Jesus Christ provided, will eventually be realized by our body, as it is presently realized by our soul, when our resurrection occurs and we receive new bodies (Rom. 8:23; 1 Cor. 15:42–55).

God does not bring His wrath to bear on all, for He differentiates between the righteous and the unrighteous, the obedient and the disobedient. He allows the righteous to finish the race (1 Cor. 9:24–27), but He reserves the right to smite the unrighteous in their course as an example that He is not only a

God of love, but also a God of justice. The children of Israel
wanted their own agenda, expecting God to cater to their wishes
as one does to a spoiled child. He certainly did not.

There are two words in the New Testament that are greatly
misunderstood because they are translated inadequately. The one
is the adjective *ékdikos* (1558) which is translated "revenger"
(Rom. 13:4) or "avenger" (1 Thess. 4:6). The Greek word is derived from the preposition *ek*, from, out of, and *díkē* (1349),
justice. It means executing righteousness and justice. The pun-
isher executes justice, not out of a sense of revenge or getting
even, but out of the sense that justice has been violated and it
must prevail. The other word is the noun *ekdíkēsis* (1557) which
is commonly translated "vengeance" (Luke 21:22; Rom. 12:19;
2 Thess. 1:8; Heb. 10:30). This means the bringing out of justice. Can you imagine what our world would be like if there were
no justice to punish the evildoer and thus curtail the wrong
which is perpetrated?

The manner in which the Israelites tested God was to believe that they could commit evil, disobey God, and experience no repercussions. Not all fell and perished, only those
who committed adultery. Not all died from the bites of the
serpents, but only those who tempted or tested God (*epeírasan*,
the third person plural aorist active indicative of *peirázō*, to
tempt or test) to see if He would do that which He said He
would do.

We must learn, from past experience, that God is a re-
warder (*misthapodótēs* [3406], a giver of what is due) of those that
seek Him, as Hebrews 11:6 proclaims. There is nothing that we
do in execution and practice of our faith in Jesus Christ for
which we will not receive a reward. We must never forget the
truth that the Apostle Paul states in 1 Thessalonians 4:6 that
"the Lord is the one who brings out justice [*ékdikos*] upon all,
such as we also have forewarned you and testified" (a.t.). And

let us also note 2 Thessalonians 1:8: "in flaming fire bringing out
justice [*ekdíkēsin*] on them that know not God, and that obey
not the gospel of our Lord Jesus Christ" (a.t.).

"And They Were Destroyed by Snakes"

But why, to give an example of God's justice, does Paul select the
incident in which the Israelites were destroyed by snakes as a result of their complaining? The preposition *hupó* (5259), by, indicates the direct agent of their destruction as being snakes.
The implication is that God can bring His justice to bear by
using any part of His creation to act upon those who disobey
Him. Satan, too, is characterized as a serpent, and it is he who
destroys us. In their sin, the Israelites yielded to Satan, and he destroyed them.

In Numbers 21:6 we read that they were bitten by fiery serpents. The adjective "fiery" is the Hebrew *śārāp̄* (8314, OT)
meaning poisonous serpents (cf. Deut. 8:15). The name for
"serpent" is *nāḥāš* (5175, OT), a snake (cf. Gen. 3:1ff.; Ex.
4:3; 7:15; 2 Kgs. 18:4). This is the most common word for a
snake and is found thirty times in the Hebrew Old Testament. Normally, the serpent is representative of evil, dating back
to the temptation of Adam and Eve in the Garden of Eden (see
Gen. 3, cf. 2 Cor. 11:3; Rev. 12:9ff.). The venom of these serpents was fatal (Num. 21:6, cf. Deut. 8:15), and their bite
must have caused an extremely painful and burning sensation.
When Israel sought deliverance, God commanded Moses to set
up a bronze figure of a serpent on a pole that those who were
bitten might look to it and live, trusting in God's healing
power. The deadly result of the bites of these snakes is referred to in Isaiah 14:29; 30:6. As to the nature of the serpent, O. Grether and W. Foerster in the *Theological Dictionary
of the New Testament–Abridged* write:

The Old Testament observes the serpent with some precision, noting its strange progression, its hissing, its sudden attacks, its dangerous bite and poison (Gen. 3:14; 49:17; Num. 21:6; Jer. 46:22;). Protection against it is a vivid metaphor for the divine protection (Ps. 91:13). It is a cunning animal that stands under God's curse (Gen. 3:1, 14, 15). It the symbolizes malignity (Deut. 32:33). It serves God when He punishes His people (Num. 21:6). In the last days, peace with the snake is one of the marks of the Messianic Kingdom (Is. 11:8).

In the New Testament the word "serpent" stands symbolically for Satan (2 Cor. 11:3 in allusion to Gen. 3:1; Rev. 12:9, 14, 15). It refers to the serpent because it eyes its objects attentively before it strikes (Matt. 7:10; Mark 16:18; Luke 10:19; 11:11; 1 Cor. 10:9; Rev. 9:19). It is used as the emblem of wisdom or cunning; for example, in a good sense in Matthew 10:16, and in a bad sense in Matthew 23:33. (See the author's *The Complete Word Study Dictionary–New Testament.*)

Paul tells us in 2 Corinthians 11:3 that in the Garden of Eden, "the serpent beguiled Eve through his subtlety," referring to the incident of Genesis 3:1–6. Its subtlety consisted of the claim that God is not going to keep His word to punish evil. Accordingly, Adam and Eve could go ahead and eat of that which God forbade and would not suffer any consequences from their actions. In other words, Satan suggested that God was a liar. Tempting God to refuse to do what He says He will do constitutes a most subtle testing of God. This original disobedience of man to God's explicit and specific command in the Garden of Eden is responsible for the fall of man. It was this act of disobedience that caused the Apostle Paul, speaking of human beings, whether Jews or Gentiles, to say, "They are all under sin; as it is written, 'there is none righteous, no, not one'" (Rom. 3:9, 10). So the example that Paul brings from this Old Testament passage in Numbers 21:4–6 is due to Adam's fall and the "some" has turned to "all" human beings. In the case of the Israelites,

God destroyed only those who disobeyed. But they disobeyed as representative of all of us who have inherited the consequence of Adam's sin. Paul writes in Romans 5:12, "Wherefore, as by one man sin entered into the world, and death by sin; and so death passed upon all men, for that all have sinned."

The Textus Receptus and the Majority Text have the verb "destroyed" in the second aorist middle indicative, that is, *apólonto,* a form of the verb *apóllumi* (622) which is derived from the preposition *apó* (575), an intensive, and *óllumi* (n.f.), to destroy. The middle voice would make it "were destroyed" (that is, the destruction was brought by themselves). The United Bible Society and the Nestle's Text have it in the imperfect middle indicative, *apóllunto,* which would literally translate "they were being destroyed." We believe *apólonto* of the Textus Receptus and the Majority Text should be preferred since in all the texts, verse 10 uses the verb in the aorist tense and not in the imperfect tense. This was not an act that was progressively taking place, but an act that took place at a definite period of time as Numbers 21:6 intimates: "And the Lord sent fiery serpents among the people, and they **bit** the people; and much people of Israel **died.**" It does not say "they **were biting**" and "people of Israel **were dying.**"

It behooves us now to examine the verb *apóllumi,* to be destroyed. Here it relates to physical death (Matt. 8:25; 26:52; Mark 4:38; Luke 8:24; 11:51; 13:33; John 18:14 [TR and MT]; Acts 5:37; 2 Cor. 4:9; 2 Pet. 3:6; Jude 11), but it can also refer to spiritual death (Matt. 10:28; Mark 1:24; Luke 4:34), that is to say, to deprive of eternal life (Luke 13:3, 5; John 3:16; 10:28; 17:12; Rom. 2:12; 1 Cor. 15:18; 2 Pet. 3:9). This spiritual death is never said to befall the believer in Jesus Christ. It is the opposite of having received life eternal.

We do find in the Scriptures, however, the expression "to sin unto death" or "a sin unto death." This is a sin in which, should a believer continue to engage, could lead him to premature physical death (see Eccl. 7:17; Jer. 14:11, 12; 34:18–20; Acts 5:1–11; 1 Cor. 11:30).

LESSONS:

1. We must never test God, but trust His Word implicitly (Gen. 3:1–7).
2. When we trust God only as to His benevolent promises, but not His predicted punishment of sin, it is as if we do not believe God at all.
3. We learn in the physical world that disobedience of natural laws has consequences which, although undesired, are certain to come; thus it is also with disobedience to the spiritual laws of God.
4. God is a God of rewards and retributions.
5. Obeying the words of Christ is the same as obeying the words of God, for Christ is God.
6. Three words stand out in this passage of Scripture in 1 Corinthians 10:1–9. The adjective *pántes*, the plural of *pás* (3956), meaning "all," and occurring in verses 1–4, stands for all humanity that is given an opportunity to escape the evil of the world around them as the Israelites were given an opportunity to escape from Egypt. The second word is the adjective occurring in verse 5, *pleíosin*, the dative plural masculine comparative form of the adjective *pleíōn*, the majority. It represents the majority of humanity that is not pleasing to God, even as the majority of the people who left Egypt did not please God. The third adjective is *tinés* (vv. 7–10), the plural form of the indefinite pronoun *tís*, some who explicitly tested God and did not believe Him. These met with physical death. The lesson here is that we can choose to turn against God, but we cannot choose whether or not we will suffer the consequences of our choice. In making a choice, we must also accept the God-imposed consequences of our choice.

1 Cor. 10:10 | *Do Not Grumble*

Neither grumble even as some of them grumbled, and they perished by the destroyer.

One characteristic of the sojourn of the Israelites through the wilderness is that God always found a way to satisfy their hunger and thirst. But in spite of the miracles He performed to meet their needs, they complained because they did not have variety or that which they had in Egypt. Their complaining was not from need, but from their desire for something other than that which God had provided.

One incident referred to that probably gave Paul reason to instruct the Corinthians not to grumble is recorded in Numbers 16 and is known as Korah's rebellion against Moses and Aaron. Korah had incited two others to align with him, Dathan and Abiram. The complainer always gets a following. What was their complaint? It is summarized in verse 13: "Is it a small thing that you have brought us up out of a land that flows with milk and honey, to kill us in the wilderness, except you make yourself altogether a prince over us?" And then they continued, "Moreover you have not brought us into a land that flows with milk and honey, or given us inheritance of fields and vineyards: will you put out the eyes of these men? We will not come up" (v. 14). They accused Moses and Aaron of having lied to them as to what they were to expect after their liberation from Egypt and accused Moses of having done what he did for the sake of personal glory. Moses became very angry (vv. 15, 25) and said in his own defense, "Hereby you shall know that the Lord has sent me to do all these works; for I have not done them of my own mind" (v. 28). The result of this rebellion was that these rebels and their followers were destroyed by fire and an earthquake which swallowed them (cf. Num. 26:6, 9; Deut. 11:6; Ps. 106:17). The noun corresponding to "grumbling" and "to grumble" is used seven times in the Septuagint in reference to Israel in the wilderness. It seems they were chronic complainers.

"Neither Grumble"

This phrase comes from *mēdé* (3366), but not, as in verses 7 to 9; *mḗ* (3361) being the relative "not," and the adversative particle *dé* (1161). The verb is the present active imperative of *goggúzō* (1111), to grumble. It means to growl in discontent in a low and indistinct voice with the idea of complaint. Some translate this as "murmur," but we feel that the word "grumble" is more accurate. It is as if the Apostle were saying, "Do not grumble at any time nor be in the habit of grumbling." In life, there will be things that occur that are not entirely to our liking, and we will be tempted to complain against such situations. The admonition of Paul, however, is that we should not allow ourselves to fall into such a habit, for in reality, we would be complaining against God, for where complaining exists, thankfulness is absent. The verb is in the second person plural and Paul is addressing the Corinthians directly. In verse 7, he commands, *mēdé gínesthe*, "do not continue" to be idolaters. He exempts himself from idolatry because he had nothing to do with it, just as he had nothing to do with grumbling and complaining.

The strict opposite of grumbling is satisfaction with whatever God gives or permits in one's life. A mother was relating to my wife an incident regarding her four-year-old who was allergic to many foods, including wheat, milk, and eggs. She had something baking in the oven, and its wonderful aroma filled the house. The boy remarked how good it smelled, and the mother sorrowfully explained that he would not be able to eat it. "But I can smell how good it is, Mommy, and I'm glad for that," he responded. What a wonderful attitude! There is one Greek adjective that describes such an attitude clearly. It is *autárkēs* (842), self-sufficient in a good sense, adequate, and consequently content. Paul, describing himself in Philippians 4:11, says, "Not that I speak in respect of want: for I have learned in whatsoever state I am, therewith to be content [*autárkēs*]." The noun is *autárkeia* (841), self-sufficiency in a good sense, sufficiency within one's self as spoken of a satisfied mind or disposition. In 2 Corinthians 9:8, Paul says, "And God is able to make all grace abound toward you; that you, always having all sufficiency in all things [*autárkeia*], may abound to every good work." He who believes he has enough is always ready and willing to help somebody else, but he who thinks he does not have enough will always seek more for himself. Writing to young Timothy in 1 Timothy 6:6, Paul says, "But godliness with contentment [*autárkeia*] is great gain." It is as if Paul gives the advice to young Timothy that one aspect of a godly character is contentment with whatever God has provided.

"Even as Some of Them Grumbled"

But why is Paul directing this imperative to the Corinthians? Because among them there existed the presence of evil partisanship. In 1 Corinthians 1:12, Paul wrote, "Now this I say, that every one of you says, I am of Paul; and I of Apollos; and I of Cephas; and I of Christ." Later, he writes, "I have planted, Apollos watered; but God gave the increase" (3:6). And in chapter 4, verse 6 he writes, "And these things, brethren, I have in a figure transferred to myself and to Apollos for your sakes; that you might learn in us not to think of men above that which is written, that no one of you be puffed up for one against another." Paul continues on in verses 18 through 21 where he writes:

> Now some are puffed up, as though I would not come to you. But I will come to you shortly, if the Lord wills, and will know, not the speech of them which are puffed up, but the power. For the kingdom of God is not in word, but in power. What will you? Shall I come unto you with a rod, or in love, and in the spirit of meekness?

As it was in the wilderness, dissatisfaction with God brought about dissatisfaction with leadership. As we read Numbers 16, we see that Korah's rebellion was concentrated upon Moses and Aaron. The rebels accused Moses and Aaron of leading the Israelites out of Egypt in order to be princes over them (v. 13).

Another accusation that Korah, Dathan, and Abiram made against their leaders was that they were lifting themselves above the congregation of the Lord. They did not want to acknowledge that Moses and Aaron assumed leadership in response to the call of God (Ex. 4:1, 10–16).

The grumblers in the wilderness would not accept the delay in the fulfillment of the promises of Moses as being part of God's plan; instead they considered them to be lies. They did not recognize that God's delays were not refusals, but blessings somehow. The delay of the Lord Jesus to go from Bethany of Perea, where John was baptizing, to Bethany of Judea, where Lazarus was sick and in need of healing, did not demonstrate neglect of duty nor disinterest, but divine providence. The Lord did not want to perform just another miracle of healing, but the miracle of the resurrection of the dead Lazarus. The Lord, in His sovereignty, could have caused the children of Israel to traverse the wilderness in a far shorter time. However, He did not because He would not, not because He could not. When Moses and Aaron undertook the leadership of bringing the children of Israel out of slavery to freedom, they did not know how long God would keep them in the wilderness, but these two anointed leaders obeyed God and did not give up.

The Lord intervened, as He always does, to eliminate Korah, Dathan, and Abiram, and those who followed them, with the punishment of death. Fourteen thousand and seven hundred people died. Grumbling brings rebellion and rebellion brings divine punishment. This is the message of 1 Corinthians 10:10. The Lord wants to arouse in us a spirit of satisfaction and thanksgiving for His provision and to disallow the spirit of complaining, for it does not remain as such, but develops into rebellion and its consequent punishment.

In the New Testament, no church equaled the example of the Philippian church. Such was Paul's satisfaction with this church that in Philippians 4:1 he wrote, "Therefore, my brethren dearly beloved and longed for, my joy and crown, so stand fast in the Lord, my dearly beloved." Such commendation is unexcelled, but yet in Philippians 2:14, Paul gave the precautionary prescription for such behavior, "Do all things without murmurings [*goggusmōn*, the genitive plural of *goggusmós* {1112}, grumbling] and disputings [*dialogismōn*, the genitive plural of *dialogismós* {1261}, mental excuses for discontent]." When one is not satisfied with God's providence, he seeks immediately to rationalize his behavior. However, it is a fact that satisfaction is never found in the quality nor quantity of material things, but in God Himself. He is the Giver of all good things, and recognition that all we have comes from Him should create in us a sense of thankfulness and satisfaction. This is the virtue of *autárkeia*, self-sufficiency in a good sense (2 Cor. 9:8; 1 Tim. 6:6; Phil. 4:11) which is realized when man relates to God as his loving Father. He considers what God directs or allows as being the expression and activity of the love of a Father's heart. Satisfaction is a matter of relationship,

not a matter of material provision. This is the true meaning of
the word "blessed" (*makários* [3107]) which presupposes that
God is not only the one who drops manna from heaven, but who
also relates His life with the life of the believer and indwells him.
The believer is thus God-satisfied and, therefore, satisfied with
what God gives in time and space.

In Jude 15, the Apostle speaks of the judgment of God:
"To execute judgment upon all, and to convince all that are ungodly among them of all their ungodly deeds which they have
ungodly committed, and of all their hard speeches which ungodly
sinners have spoken against Him." The punishment of God is
certain to come upon ungodly deeds. But how do ungodly deeds
arise? He tells us in verse 16, "These are murmurers [*goggustaí*,
the plural of *goggustēs* {1113}, grumbler, found only this one
time in the entire New Testament], complainers, walking after
their own lusts; and their mouths speak great swelling words,
having men's persons in admiration because of advantage" (a.t.).
Grumbling starts with the spirit of dissatisfaction, and dissatisfaction starts when self is in the center instead of God.

"And They Died by the Destroyer"

The Apostle Paul, having referenced the destruction of those who
rebelled under the leadership of Korah, says, "And they died
by the destroyer." The word "destroyer" translates the Greek
noun *olothreutēs* (3644). This is the only place it occurs in the
New Testament. This noun, pertaining to the one who destroys,
is related to the noun *ólethros* (3639), destruction, which comes
from the verb *óllumi* (n.f.) which means to destroy or kill. The
noun is used only of divine punishment (1 Cor. 5:5; 1 Thess. 5:3;
2 Thess. 1:9; 1 Tim. 6:9; Sept.: Prov. 21:7). The verb *óllumi*,
which is not found by itself in the New Testament, occurs as the
compound *apóllumi* (622), to destroy. In 1 Timothy 6:9 the two
words occur together. The word *ólethros* is translated "destruc-

tion," and the word *apṓleia* (684) is translated "perdition," which is derived from the verb *apóllumi*. The difference between the two words is elaborated upon under the word *apṓleia* in the author's *The Complete Word Study Dictionary—New Testament* (p. 246) as follows:

> *Ólethros* refers to the actual physical death of those who desire to be rich by any means, such as Judas, Ananias and Sapphira. . . . and speaks more of the way in which destruction comes than of the state in which a lost person is found. It refers specifically to the destruction of the flesh (1 Cor. 5:5). *Apṓleia,* on the other hand, refers to the destruction or perishing of the whole personality as is indicated by the opposite of *apóllumi* which is *sṓzomai* (4982), to be saved, "that the spirit might be saved." Thus we can conclude that for the flesh there is *ólethros,* while for the spirit there is salvation. Yet salvation may be taken as the antonym of both *apóllumi* and *ólethros.* In the latter case, the word "salvation" must be taken as the healing of the body (James 5:15, where the word translated "saved" is the Greek word *sṓzō,* [4982] to save). In the spiritual realm, however, *sṓzō* is also the opposite of *apóllumi* to perish. Thus *sōtēría* (4991), salvation or deliverance, can be taken as the exact opposite of *apṓleia.*

In 1 Timothy 6:9 we read, "But they that will be rich fall into temptation and a snare, and into many foolish and hurtful lusts, which drown men in destruction [*ólethron,* the accusative of *ólethros* which means physical death] and perdition [*apṓleian,* the accusative of *apṓleia* which means the loss of the whole personality—body, soul, and spirit]." *Apṓleia* refers to the state after death wherein exclusion from salvation is a realized fact, and where man, instead of becoming what he might have been, is lost and ruined. *Ólethros* then refers to the first death and *apṓleia* refers to the second death, which is eternal exclusion from Christ's kingdom.

The verb "died" in the Textus Receptus, the Majority Text, Nestle, and UBS in verse 10 is *apṓlonto,* the third person plural second aorist middle indicative of *apóllumi* to be lost, to perish.

The verb is used exactly the same in verse 9 in the Textus Receptus and the Majority Text, speaking of the disposition of those who tempted God, and it is in the middle voice which indicates that they brought about their own death and final destiny. It refers not only to the fact that they died because they deserved to, but also that they were forever separated from the joy and presence of God which they could have enjoyed had they believed. The same happened to the grumblers. They died because they deserved to and were excluded from the eternal salvation of God. The fact that the verb is in the aorist tense means that once a decision of death and perdition is made, it is irreversible. The punishment that God allows to come upon sin is simply the foreannounced consequence of sin. It confirms the irreversible law of reaping that which one sows. Again, we must emphasize the fact that God created us in His own image with the ability to choose, but He did not give us the privilege of choosing the consequences of our choice. In these three verses, 8, 9, and 10, we find the choices that man made to engage in sexual sin, to tempt God, and to grumble. The eternal Law of God is that "the wages of sin is death; but the gift of God is eternal life through Jesus Christ our Lord" (Rom. 6:23). To tempt God is to reject the veracity of His Word.

LESSONS:

1. Grumbling may be a silent or barely audible complaint against God.
2. This dissatisfaction springs from having self as the center of one's life instead of God.
3. Dissatisfaction should be nipped in the bud and should be replaced by thanksgiving always, for all things (Eph. 5:20).
4. Grumbling leads to revolt, and revolt against God has eternal consequences.
5. Physical death is bad enough, but not as bad as eternal separation from God.

1 Cor. 10:11

History Was Recorded for Our Instruction

> *Now all these things were taking place as examples one after the other to them, and they were recorded for the proper setting of our mind for whom the ends of the ages finally arrived.*

In verse 6, the Apostle Paul tells us that the things which happened to the Israelites became examples for us so that we would not imitate them in lusting after evil things. In this verse, Paul tells us that history was consecutively recorded that it might have an effect upon us. From the negative of verse 6, Paul now moves to a positive mind-set.

"Now *All These* Things Were Taking Place as Examples One After the Other"

The word "examples" (*túpoi* [5179]) which occurs here in verse 11, is the same word found in verse 6. However, Paul adds the adjective "all" (*pánta*, the nominative plural neuter form of the adjective *pás* [3956], all) which is missing from verse 6. This is found in the Textus Receptus and Majority Text, but is missing from the critical texts (UBS and Nestle's Text). Its presence shows us that all the events which took place by the direction or permission of God had a useful purpose for our learning. Paul confirms this in Romans 8:28 by saying that "**All** things work together for good to them that love God." A wise person ponders and prays over all Scripture to determine its application to his life.

Whereas the verb used in verse 6 is *egenḗthēsan* (1096), took place, we find that an entirely different verb is used in verse 11. It is *sunébainon*, were taking place, the third person plural imperfect active indicative of *sumbaínō* (4819) which is derived from the conjunction *sún* (4862), conjointly together, and *baínō*, meaning to walk, to come about. The word *baínō* is not found in the New Testament. It refers to the events of the wilderness sojourn as having taken place one after the other, and putting them all together, they become lessons in their totality from which we should learn. Hence, we have chosen to translate the verb as "were taking place." It definitely is distinguished from *egenḗthēsan* which simply means "they became." By using the verb *sunébainon*, we understand that God is sovereign and He has a purpose and a goal in all that He directs or permits in our lives. Things do not just happen. God permits them for our instruction.

"To Them"

This phrase "to them" is translated from *ekeínois*, the dative plural masculine form of the demonstrative pronoun *ekeínos* (1565), that one. The Apostle uses the phrase "to them" to show us that there are lessons for us to learn, just as there were for the Israelites. Although those events took place many years ago, they are definitely related to our present life and our future destiny. Madame Chiang Kai-shek said, "We live in the present, we dream of the future, but we learn eternal truths from the past." And again, as Oliver Wendell Holmes, Jr., declared, "A page of history is worth a volume of logic."

"And They Were Recorded"

God saw to it that not only the good things were recorded in the history of Israel, but also the bad. He recorded them in writing so that they would not become distorted through passing generations, but remain as clear examples for years to come that all may know the will and workings of God. The word for "recorded" is *egráphē*, the third person singular second aorist passive indicative of *gráphō* (1125), to write.

"For the Proper Setting of Our Mind"

This record has been given to us for a purpose which is the "proper setting of our minds" (*prós nouthesían* [*prós* {4314}, toward, for the purpose of; *nouthesían*, the accusative feminine of the noun *nouthesía* {3559}, setting of the mind, which is derived from *noús* {3563}, mind, and *thésis* (n.f.), placing, from the verb *tithēmi* {5087}, to place]). This compound noun is usually translated "admonition" or "exhortation." It is any word of encouragement or reproof which leads to correct behavior and results in a proper mind-setting. The noun occurs in 1 Corinthians 10:11; Ephesians 6:4 and Titus 3:10. The verb *noutheteō* (3560) occurs in Acts 20:31; Romans 15:14; 1 Corinthians 4:14; Colossians 1:28; 3:16; 1 Thessalonians 5:12, 14, and 2 Thessalonians 3:15. The Apostle Paul lets us know that our minds must be set on a path that is pleasing to the Lord and under control. As a little child must learn to control himself, so must we in our Christian walk.

Things did not simply happen to the Israelites as a result of chance. This is why we did not translate the verb *sunébainon* as "happened," for that connotes chance or caprice. Everything that God allowed had its basis on the decisions and the actions of the Israelites. That preposition *sún*, together or with, forming the prefix in the verb *sumbaínō,* relates the idea of reaping and sowing, so to speak, where the action of God constituted a response to man's provocation of disobedience. The Israelites ought to have noted this truth and learned from it. This is why the Apostle Paul said they should have become examples "to them" (*ekeínois*), that is, to the Israelites. For us, however, these events were recorded so that our minds might be steadied and firmly set which is indicated by the noun *nouthesía*. It is evident from recorded history that God responds to the decisions and actions of men. He wants us to learn that we cannot disobey and expect Him to disregard it. God's actions are either rewards for obedience or retribution or chastisement for disobedience.

It is not only physical death which may result from sin, but also spiritual death or separation from God. This idea is intrinsic in the verb *apólonto*, the third person plural in the aorist middle indicative of *apóllumi* (612), to perish, of verses 9 and 10. It means lost forever as far as the salvation of the Lord is concerned. The ones who have a spiritual relationship with God do not test Him, but believe His Word as it is recorded.

What is it that our minds must be set upon? It is the judgment of God as it was meted out to the Israelites as they left Egypt and dwelt in the wilderness for forty years. If we are going to be morally feeble, as they were (v. 6), we, too, shall fall (v. 8). We cannot test God and grumble, disregarding His abundant and miraculous care of us, and experience no repercussions. The eternal law of sowing and reaping stated by the Apostle Paul in Galatians 6:7 holds firm: "Be you not deceived; God is not mocked: for whatever a man sows, that shall he also reap." One difficulty in fully comprehending this law is that in the physical world it does not always take long to reap the results of that which we sow. If we disobey the law of gravity and decide to test it and throw ourselves from a high place, we shall instantly be injured or even killed. If we touch fire, we shall be burned immediately. But when we disobey the spiritual laws of God, His mercifulness and long-suffering enter into the picture. In His mercy, He postpones the results of our spiritual disobedience. While nothing may seem to happen by rejecting the salvation of God, the end result is perdition (*apóleia* [684]). This comes at the end of our lives and the resurrection unto judgment (John 5:29). The judgment of God is twofold. Believers, at the coming of the Lord, will experience a resurrection unto life, but unbelievers will experience a resurrection unto judgment. Believers will be judged for their works when they appear before the judgment seat of Christ to receive the rewards for that which they did during their lifetime (2 Cor. 5:10), but unbelievers will face God to receive the retribution of their evil works (Rev. 20:13).

Both unbelievers and believers have a mind (*noús*, intellect) with which they determine their eternal destiny. Paul, in Romans 1:28, writes: "And even as they did not like to retain God in their knowledge [*epígnōsis* {1922}, recognition, superknowledge], God gave them over to a reprobate mind [*adókimon*, the accusative of *adókimos* {96}, unapproved, the same word as we find in 1 Cor. 9:27; *noún*, the accusative of *noús*, mind, intellect], to do those things which are not convenient [*kathēkonta*, the proper things, the accusative plural neuter present active participle of the verb *kathēkō* {2520}, to be proper, becoming]." Thus unbelievers are responsible for allowing their minds to lead them to do those things that are improper. These unbelievers, besides receiving the basic punishment of living eternally apart from God, will suffer variably according to their individual evil works (Rev. 20:13). On the other hand, believers are "approved" (*dókimoi*, the plural of *dókimos* [1384], acceptable, approved [2 Cor. 13:7]). There are degrees of acceptability, however, according to the works done during our lives (1 Cor. 3:10–15; 2 Cor. 5:10; 2 Tim. 2:15; James 1:12). We as believers are said to have the "mind of Christ" (1 Cor. 2:16). As such, we are responsible for every word and every deed (James 2:12, 13), for we intuitively know right from wrong.

"For Whom"

"For whom" (*eis* [1519], for, unto; *hoús*, the accusative plural masculine form of the relative pronoun *hós* [3739], who) refers to the contemporaries of the Apostle Paul, that is, the Christians who lived in Corinth and for whose admonition he wrote this epistle. However, "All Scripture is given by inspiration of God, and is profitable for doctrine, for reproof, for correction, for instruction in righteousness: that the man of God may be perfect, thoroughly furnished unto all good works" (2 Tim. 3:16, 17). Thus it applies to us as well, and it behooves us to pay close attention for we are without excuse.

"The Ends of the Ages"

In order to arrive at the proper meaning of this phrase, we must look into the definitive meaning of each word individually and then conjoined.

The first word we must examine is *télē*, the nominative plural neuter form of the noun *télos* (5056). It has a variety of meanings. As we definitely see from Luke 22:37, one meaning is "fulfillment": "For I say unto you, that this that is written must yet be accomplished [*telesthḗnai*, the aorist passive infinitive of *teléō* {5055}, to complete, execute, conclude or accomplish] in Me, 'And He was reckoned among the transgressors': for the things concerning Me have an end." This last word, "end" or *télos*, means the fulfillment, the accomplishment. It can also mean "tax" or "tribute" (Matt. 17:25; Rom. 13:7). Another meaning of the word *télos* is "goal" (1 Tim. 1:5; 1 Pet. 1:9, etc.). In 1 Corinthians 10:11 we must give it the meaning of "goal" or "aim" or "purpose." However, uniquely here in verse 11, the word occurs in the plural, *tá télē*. *Tá* is the nominative plural neuter article of *ho* (3588), the. Everywhere else it occurs in the singular, *tó télos*. Thus Paul must refer to the goals or the purposes of each age. In agreement with the word *télē*, ends or fulfillments, the word *aiṓn* (165) occurs in the plural, that is, "the ends of the ages [*aiṓnōn*, the genitive plural masculine noun]." And so Paul is speaking here of the goals or purposes of the various periods of time known as ages. It is clear that the Apostle distinguishes between the age of Israel, before the Messiah came, and this present age (2 Cor. 4:4). This is the age of the kingdom of God, invisibly established in the hearts of men. There is yet another period of time coming in which the kingdom of God will be established visibly (Luke 17:20–24). So we have the age before Christ, the age during Christ's presence on earth physically and spiritually, and the period of time that will follow this age of grace, and that is the period of the judgment of God. Each of these periods of time has a specific end.

In the prophetic Olivet Discourse, we find our Lord speaking of the "consummation of the age [*sunteleías* {4930}, consummation, entire completion; *toú*, of the; *aiṓnos*, age]" (Matt. 24:3, cf. 13:39, 40, 49). In Matthew 28:20 the Lord does not speak about the end of the world, but about the completion of the final age. Therefore, the age of Christ began with the announcement of His descent to the earth and continues until the time He completes the purposes for which He came.

In the parable of the wheat and the tares, we find the Lord referring to the consummation of the age as the time of the ultimate punishment of the tares which represent unbelievers (Matt. 13:40). Likewise, in the parable of the dragnet, the consummation of the age refers to the time of separation between believers and unbelievers (Matt. 13:47–49).

In Hebrews 9:26 we have the phrase in the plural form, "the consummation of the ages." The literal translation of this verse is, "For then He should have suffered many times from the

foundation of the world; but now once at the consummation of
the ages, He has appeared to put away sin through the sacrifice
of Himself." It is extremely important for us to understand this
verse in view of the fact that the sacrifice of Jesus Christ was sufficient for all ages; that is, for the period of Israel before the
coming of the Lord in the flesh, for the period of His incarnation and the establishment of His kingdom in the hearts of
people, and for the period after the Messiah left the world with
a definitive promise to return (Acts 1:11). Although Jesus came
as the God-Man at a specific time in history to die for the sins
of the world, He died for everyone irrespective of time, that
whoever believes on Him at any time will have everlasting life
(John 3:16). This is why Christ could tell the Jews of His day,
"Your father Abraham rejoiced to see My day: and he saw it, and
was glad" (John 8:56). Jesus Christ is the central figure for
the redemption of mankind. This is the reason that Paul, in
1 Corinthians 10:9, says, "Neither let us continue to tempt
Christ [who was eternally with God the Father], as some of
them also tempted, and were destroyed by serpents." Temptation
against God is temptation against Christ, and temptation against
Christ is temptation against God the Father.

"Finally Arrived"

The verb that indicates the arrival of the end of the ages is one that
is difficult to translate. It is the verb *katéntēsen*, the third person
singular aorist active indicative of *katantáō* (2658), to finally arrive. It is derived from the preposition *katá* (2596), down (or it may
be used as an intensive), and *antáō* meaning "to meet." This word
is not found by itself in the New Testament. The verb is used to
indicate the physical arrival at a place (Acts 16:1; 18:19, 24;
20:15; 21:7; 25:13; 26:7; 27:12; 28:13). It is found four times in
a somewhat metaphorical meaning, implying a one-sided final arrival. Here in 1 Corinthians 10:11, it refers to the consummation

of the goals of the ages. In the Textus Receptus and Majority Text the verb is in the aorist, *katéntesen,* which would translate "finally arrived," or in the perfect tense of the critical text, *katénteken,* "has arrived and is already here." The aorist or perfect tense is used in order to indicate that the imminence of the end is present.

Not only the imminence of the coming judgment is implied here, but also the suddenness of it. The words of Christ in Luke 21:34 demand our careful attention: "And take heed to yourselves, lest at any time your hearts be overcharged with surfeiting and drunkenness, and cares of this life, and so that day come upon you unawares [*aiphnídios* {160}, unexpected, sudden]." The verb is used with similar meaning by Paul in Philippians 3:11 where he is speaking about the resurrection from the dead (*exanástasis* [1815]), or a better translation would be "a resurrection out of the dead": "If by any means I might attain [*katantéso*] unto the resurrection [*exanástasin*] out of the dead." It was going to be a sudden and imminent event, as described in 1 Thessalonians 4:13–18. Thus all mankind will experience the end of the ages, which in its eschatological meaning implies final judgment. We, as Christians, are to behave as if the judgment is just around the corner. Let not the judgment of God take us unaware.

LESSONS:

1. Paul records the history of Israel so that we may learn from it.
2. He recounts the behavior of the children of Israel in the wilderness in the face of the adequate and miraculous provision of God so that they may be deprived of any excuse for their misbehavior.
3. Nothing that takes place in history is a matter of chance. We should evaluate calamities in view of our behavior.
4. The state of our mind is important, and history should teach us how to think clearly.
5. The judgments of God are recorded so that we may learn how suddenly and how surely they come as a result of human behavior.
6. The final coming of Christ will be sudden.

1 Cor. 10:12 | *A Warning for the One Who Thinks He Stands*

So then, let him who thinks he has been standing securely beware lest he fall.

In view of the eschatological judgment and evaluation of mankind, it is necessary that we have a true estimate of ourselves and not a false one. Our presumption of strength may prove disastrous to us if we are found wanting. We will do well to heed the words of our Master, who in Matthew 7:21–23 said,

> Not every one that says unto me, "Lord, Lord," shall enter into the kingdom of heaven: but he that does the will of My Father which is in heaven. Many will say to Me in that day, "Lord, Lord, have we not prophesied in Your name? and in Your name have cast out devils? and in Your name done many wonderful works?" And then will I profess unto them, "I never knew you: depart from Me, you who work iniquity."

Verse 12 is a call to individual self-examination. In the previous verses we had the plural used:

> ". . . to the intent **we** should not lust after evil things . . ." (v. 6).

> Neither **be you** [*gínesthe,* the second person plural present imperative of the verb *gínomai* {1097}, to be, become] idolaters . . ." (v. 7).

> "Neither "**let us** commit fornication . . ." (v. 8).

"Neither **let us** tempt Christ . . ." (v. 9)

"Neither **murmur you** [*goggúzete,* the second person plural present imperative of *goggúzō* {1111}, to murmur, grumble] . . ." (v. 10).

"Now all these things happened unto **them** for examples . . ." (v. 11).

Now Paul has shifted to the singular, as if to place individual responsibility upon the one who thinks that he stands securely. He says, "So then **let him** who thinks **he** has been standing. . . ." Who does Paul have in mind? He is thinking of the person who considers himself strong enough to sit in the midst of idolaters and enjoy the meat at the idol temple (1 Cor. 8:10), who thinks that he stands so firmly that he can disregard his environment. The Apostle Paul wants us to use our minds, to think carefully, and not to simply suppose that we are well-grounded. We are to make sure of our foundation.

"So Then"

The conjunction *hṓste* (5620), so then, connects the preceding verses with the ones following. The same conjunction is used in 1 Corinthians 4:5; 11:33; 14:39; 15:58. It is always used to add emphasis and to draw our attention to what follows. If that which happened to Israel in the past is a lesson for us, let us pay close attention to this Scripture, for "history is recorded so that we may avoid the errors of the past."

"Let Him Who Thinks"

This phrase is translated from *ho dokṓn,* the nominative singular masculine present active participle of *dokéō* (1380), to think, imagine, to have a subjective estimate or opinion of oneself. It is a verb from which we have the adjective *dókimos* (1384), acceptable, proved, and it is the opposite of *adókimos* (96), unacceptable, unapproved. The verb *dokṓn* in this verse is used merely subjectively. It refers to what one thinks of himself, which may not be a reality at all. Pride is deceitful. Paul wrote in 2 Timothy 2:15, "Study to show yourself approved [*dókimon*] unto God." God is the only One who can judge us rightly. In the illustration of the athlete which Paul gave in 1 Corinthians 9:24–27, he said ". . . lest that by any means, when I have preached to others, I myself should be a castaway [*adókimos*, unacceptable, unapproved]." The examination of self, to see whether we are indeed approved and acceptable, is discussed by the Apostle Paul in 2 Corinthians 13:5–7:

> Examine yourselves, whether you be in the faith; prove your own selves. Know you not your own selves, how that Jesus Christ is in you, except you be reprobates [*adókimoi*]? But I trust that you shall know that we are not reprobates [*adókimoi*]. Now I pray to God that you do no evil; not that we should appear approved [*dókimoi*], but that you should do that which is honest, though we be as reprobates [*adókimoi*].

As Paul says in Romans 12:3, "For I say, through the grace given unto me, to every man that is among you, not to think of himself more highly than he ought to think; but to think soberly, according as God has dealt to every man the measure of faith."

"He Has Been Standing *Securely*"

We have added the adverb "securely" to the verb "standing" (*hestánai*, the perfect active infinitive of *hístēmi* [2476], to stand) as it is implied that the warning is not merely for the person who thinks that he stands, but for the one that thinks his stand is secure. The verb *hístēmi* is used in the absolute sense with the verb *pésē*, the third person singular second aorist active subjunctive of *píptō* (4098), to fall. The danger is in thinking that one is standing securely and can run the race well that God has set before him, that he is strong enough and does not need to practice or exercise self-control (1 Cor. 9:25). It is as if Paul were saying, Do not run the race if you are running on presumed strength. You will fall during your race and put to shame the name of Christ and His strength which you think you have. This does not concern, in any way, salvation and the new birth as given by Jesus Christ, but the presumption of having been saved.

The words "stand" and "fall" are also found in Romans 14:4: "Who are you that judges another man's servant? To his own master he **stands** or **falls**. Yes, he shall be held up: for God is able to make him stand." The thesis of the Apostle Paul is that God does His part in enabling us to stand. But this does not absolve us of our personal responsibility to keep ourselves from places where we can slip and fall from the position that God has given us to maintain. This position is one of a runner in a race who can advance but must watch carefully lest there be danger in his path that might cause him to trip. Romans 14:5 assigns the responsibility to the individual: "Let each man [*hékastos* {1538}, each one individually] in his own mind [*noí*, the dative singular masculine form of the noun *noús* {3563}, mind, the single word making up the compound word *nouthesía* {3559}, the setting of the mind] be fully persuaded [*plērophoreísthō*, the third person singular present passive imperative of *plērophoréō* {4135}, to persuade fully or to be fully assured]." Paul wants us not to simply **think** that we stand, but to **be certain** that we do. He who merely thinks he stands may fall, but he who is solidly grounded on the Lord Jesus Christ will not fall.

"Beware Lest He Fall"

The literal meaning of this phrase is, "Let him watch out not to fall." The Greek construction is *blepétō*, the third person singular present active imperative of *blépō* (991), to see, to heed, beware; *mḗ* (3361), the relative "not" as contrasted to the absolute "not" (*ou* [3756]); *pésē*, the third person singular second aorist active subjunctive of *píptō*, to fall. This has nothing to do with God's work of grace in one's heart. Rather, it means to fall short of that which one could be if he accepted God's desire for him. We so commonly think of falling from grace as meaning to lose one's salvation that we apply that terminology here also. This has nothing to do with man annulling the grace of God. One Scripture that has been misinterpreted to suggest that we may fall from grace is Galatians 5:4: "Christ is become of no effect unto you, whoever of you are justified by the law; you are fallen from grace." The verb used for "fallen" here (TR and MT) is not the basic verb *píptō*, to fall, but *exepésate*, the second person plural aorist active indicative of the compound verb *ekpíptō* (1601), to fall from or out of (*ex* [1537], out of; and *píptō*). Paul's argument here is, "Christ has become of no effect unto you, whoever of you are justified by the law." It is either the law that justified you or grace. You have fallen away from the clear teaching of Christ. It cannot be both. If it is the law, then you are not depending on the grace which God has provided and grace has no meaning to you since the law supposedly has proven sufficient. If it is by grace that you are saved, then the law had nothing to do with your salvation. But 1 Corinthians 10:12 does not say *ekpésē*, shall fall out of grace, but simply *pésē*, fall, without an adjunct. Beware not to fall in your walk due to in-adequate preparation and lack of self-control (1 Cor. 9:25).

That it is possible to fall is implied by the relative "not" (*mē*). This fall is of man's own making and not because of a di-vine forsaking of the one who has been saved by Christ. The re-demption that Christ secured for us through His blood is an eternal redemption (Heb. 9:12). The life God gives as a result of believing in Christ is not temporary life, but eternal life (John 3:16). Christ said in John 10:28, "And I give unto them eternal life; and they shall never [*ou*, the absolute 'not,' representing God's responsibility, followed by *mē*, the relative 'not,' indicat-ing man's responsibility] perish, neither shall any man pluck them out of My hand." And then in verse 29, our Lord says, "My

Father, which gave them Me, is greater than all; and no man is able to pluck them out of My Father's hand."

While it is possible for someone running the race to fall, it is not a fatal fall, but a recoverable one (1 John 1:9, 10; 2:1, 2). But far better than falling and being recovered is to avert the fall altogether through personal discipline and self-control (1 Cor. 9:25).

LESSONS:

1. We should never judge ourselves based on our own standards, but in the light of the standard that God has set for us.
2. We must never think of ourselves as being so secure that we can be comfortable in environments which could lead us into sin.
3. Verse 12 has nothing to do with the salvation given by Christ which joins us to His body (1 Cor. 12:13).
4. This warning is given primarily for those believers who thought they were so strong they could participate in the feasts of sacrifices by idolaters. These were not merely banquets, but were accompanied by immoral orgies. By so doing, they were exposing themselves to the danger of individual sin. Although there can be repentance, confession, and forgiveness of sin (1 John 1:9), it is better to avoid the sin in the first place.

1 Cor. 10:13

God Will Not Permit Testing beyond Endurance

Absolutely no testing has overtaken you which does not pertain to mankind, but God is trustworthy who absolutely will not permit you to be tested beyond what you are able to endure, but will, together with the testing, provide the way out.

In 1 Corinthians 10:9 we were admonished not to test Christ as some of the Israelites tested God and fell in their wilderness journey. We were admonished also in verse 12 to be careful lest thinking we are invulnerable to sin, we fall. Here in verse 13, Paul encourages us regarding our human propensity to sin.

"No Testing"

It is always problematic whether to translate the Greek word *peirasmós* (3986) as "temptation" or "testing." Only by the context can we determine the correct translation. This verse is the only one in the Corinthian epistles in which the noun *peirasmós* occurs along with the verb *peirasmós* (3985).

This same word *peirázō* is also found in 1 Corinthians 7:5 where the Apostle Paul, in speaking of the marriage relationship, says to be careful lest Satan would tempt you, and in 2 Corinthians 13:5 where we find it translated as "examine yourselves" (*peirázete*). It has the general meaning of "test yourselves." Except for 1 Corinthians 7:5, where it is stated that Satan is "tempting" us, in all the other references both the noun and the verb mean "testing" and "test." With the exception of these latter two references, in all the other passages the one who tests us is God. For this reason we have translated the word *peirasmós* in 1 Corinthians 10:13 as "testing" and not "temptation."

Both the noun and the verb derive from the word *peíra* (3984), experience, trial, and the only places *peíra* is found are Hebrews 11:29, 36. When the purpose of testing is for us to acquire experience, then God is the author. He is testing us to determine if we can handle greater responsibility. God considers testing necessary, not to lead us into an evil act, but to acquire experience and strength. If you have wondered why God has not entrusted you with greater responsibility, is it possible that you have tried to avoid His testing? Whenever Satan tests us, the word should be translated "tempts," because his purpose is to cause us to fail, to fall into sin. It is never God's desire to tempt us to sin, and for this reason the Lord taught us in His prayer to say, "Lead us not into temptation" (Matt. 6:13). The word *peirasmós* here should be translated "testing." Usually we have the wrong perception of the necessity of testing by God. In our prayers we should be honest and confess our aversion to testing.

"Has Overtaken You"

In this life, both Christians and non-Christians come face to face with testings. For the non-Christians, testings become occasions to sin, but for Christians, they become occasions for training (*paideía* [3809]). Sometimes, though, the Christian feels the testings may be too severe and beyond his ability to bear. Paul had Christians in mind when he wrote our verse, "No testing has overtaken **you**." The "no" is expressed by the absolute negative *ou* (3756) in connection with the verb "overtaken" (*eílēphen*, third person singular perfect active indicative of *lambánō* [2983], to take, seize, lay hold of, which has the idea of force or violence). Paul wants us to know that God has not allowed any believer to be tested beyond his ability to bear as His child. Implied also is the sense of surprise.

"Which Does Not Pertain to Mankind"

What is translated as "which does not" is the expression *ei mḗ* (1508), if not, except. This expression is made up of *ei* (1487), the suppositional subjective conjunction "if," and *mḗ* (3361), the relative "not." Our testing is only that which is common to humanity, Paul says. The adjective *anthrṓpinos* (442) means "pertaining to humanity." *Ánthrōpos* (444) is the Greek word for "man" or "human being," and the suffix *inos* means "pertaining to the nature of" (1 Cor. 2:13; 4:3). God recognizes, at all times, that we are only human and cannot endure testing beyond human ability. There is no doubt that God takes our nature into consideration when He tests us. Psalm 87:6 tells us that "The Lord shall count, when He writes up the people, that this man was born there." In other words, God takes into consideration every detail about each person.

Noteworthy is Hebrews 4:15: "For we have not a high priest which cannot be touched with the feeling of our infirmities; but in all points having had the experience [*pepeiraménon*, MT] the same as we have, yet without sin." The Majority Text has the verb *peiráō* (3987), to have the experience (*peíra*) versus *pepeirasménon* from *peirázō*, to tempt or to test, of the Textus Receptus and critical texts.

"But God *Is* Trustworthy"

God, however, knowing our nature and our ability to bear the tests that He permits in our lives, will not go beyond our level of endurance, as we read in His dealings with Job and David (1 Chr. 21:1; 2 Sam. 24:1). The adjective *pistós* (4103) has the objective meaning of "trustworthy." God can be trusted in our testing. Paul stresses God's faithfulness in his Corinthian epistles (1 Cor. 1:9; 10:13; 2 Cor. 1:18). The word "trustworthy" is found repeatedly also in 1 Timothy 1:15; 3:1; 4:9; 2 Tim. 2:11; and Titus 3:8. It is encouraging to note that the definite article *ho* (3588), the, precedes the noun *Theós* (2316), thus referring to God **the** Father (John 1:1b, 2). God never makes a mistake in His testing. He never allows it to be less than we need to encourage our growth nor more than we can bear.

"Who Absolutely Will Not Permit You"

This phrase is translated from the Greek *hós* (3739), who; *ouk*, the absolute negative "not"; *eásei*, the third person singular future active indicative of *eáō* (1439), to permit, allow; *humás* (5209), you. The promise of God is absolute!

In Acts 16:7, we find that both verbs *peirázō*, to test or try, and *eáō*, to permit, are used. Speaking of the Apostle Paul and his companions, Luke says, "After they were come to Mysia, they attempted [*epeírazon*, the third person plural imperfect active indicative of *peirázō*, to try, to attempt] to go into Bithynia: but the Spirit suffered them not [*eíasen*, the third person singular aorist active indicative of *eáō*, to permit]." Here Paul and his companions were trying to spread the gospel to further areas of Asia. Although this was commendable, we find that the Holy Spirit did not permit them to do so. He placed limitations as to where they were to go and what they were to do. It is good to remember that while God limits the powers of those who would test us, He also places limitations on our own plans, even though we may think that what we are doing brings glory to God.

"To Be Tested"

The word *peirasthḗnai* is the aorist passive infinitive of *peirázō* which, as we explained in this instance, ought to be translated "tested" and not "tempted." God does not tempt us to sin. As James 1:13, 14 says, "Let no man say when he is tempted, 'I am tempted of God': for God cannot be tempted with evil, neither tempts He any man: But every man is tempted, when he is drawn away of his own lust, and enticed." That refers to both direct and indirect temptation. God only allows testing to come into our lives in order to strengthen us. A teacher or professor gives tests not only to determine what a person has learned, but to motivate him to deeper study and retention.

"Beyond What You Are Able to Endure"

This phrase is translated from the Greek *hupér* (5228), above, beyond; *hó*, the accusative singular neuter form of the relative pronoun *hós*, that which, what; *dúnasthe*, the second person plural present middle deponent indicative of *dúnamai* (1410), to be able. What we translated "to endure" is *hupenegkeín*, the second aorist active infinitive of *hupophérō* (5297). This is derived from *hupó* (5259), under, and *phérō* (5342), to bring, to bear. The endurance level of every believer is known only to God, and we are assured that He will never allow us to be tested to the breaking point. Every test purposes to make us more dependable and firm in our faith.

"But Will, Together with the Testing, Provide the Way Out"

Here we have the Greek word *allá* (235), but; *poiḗsei*, the third person singular future active indicative of *poiéō* (4160), to make, expressing action either as completed or continued. The result of every test is a particular accomplishment of God in the life of each individual believer. It will be either something completed in itself, or it will be something that will lead to a completed accomplishment.

God has the ability to use each test as the means to an end. The conjunction that is used which would be translated "along with" is *sún* (4862), conjointly together. Paul implies here that without testing, God would not be able to accomplish that which He desires in the life of the believer.

"With the testing" comes from *tō*, with the, dative singular neuter of the article *ho* (3588), and *peirasmō*, dative singular masculine form of the noun *peirasmós*, testing. The literal translation of *kaí* (2532), "and" or "also," thus relates the testing with "the way out."

It is to be noted that the two conjunctions, *sún*, along with or together with, and *kaí*, and, also, are used in the sentence, "But will **along** with the testing, **also** provide a way out." This indicates that the same One who directs or permits the testing, also will make a way out of that particular testing. There is no doubt that the One who provides the way out is the Lord; therefore the word *peirasmós* must be assigned the meaning of "testing" and not of "temptation," because God tempts no man.

The word which is commonly translated "escape" and which we have elected to translate "the way out" is the Greek word *ékbasis* (1545), a going out or a way to escape, an exit from a house, found only here and in Hebrews 13:7. The word is derived from *ek* (1537), out of, and *básis* (939), a basis, and the verb *baínō*, to go. The meaning of the word *ékbasis* is more apparent in its use in Hebrews 13:7: "Remember them which have the rule over you, who have spoken unto you the Word of God: whose faith follow, considering the end [*ékbasin*, the accusative of *ékbasis*, outcome, result] of their conversation [conduct]." The Apostle is saying here that we should remember the conduct which resulted from the faith of the Christians who ruled over us. Their conduct is spoken of as the result or the outcome of their faith. Faith that is real will certainly affect behavior.

Likewise, every testing that God allows in our lives will have some result, some outcome which is related to the testing. It is to be noted that the word *ékbasin* in 1 Corinthians 10:13 has the definite article in front of it, "But will, together with the testing, provide **the** way out." He speaks here of the beneficence of every testing that He directs or permits in our lives.

What is the specific purpose of the testing allowed by God? It is expressed by an infinitive with the genitive article, *toú dúnasthai*, the present middle deponent infinitive of *dúnamai*, to be able. This genitive form of the article with the infinitive is equivalent to the conjunction of purpose *hína* (2443), so that. The verb *dúnamai* has the meaning of being able to accomplish, and not simply to be made inherently strong, which would be indicated by the use of the verb *ischúō* (2480), to be strengthened. The implied meaning is that with every test we pass through, God gives us the ability to emerge victorious, thus we progress in our Christian walk.

The Apostle does not promise that the Lord will spare us from testing and suffering. Every test has its corresponding way out and victory. Christ did not suffer because of any sin of His own, but for our sins (2 Cor. 5:21). We, as His disciples, are never saved from suffering, but rejoice in suffering because Christ's strength is manifest in our suffering. If we are faithful to Him, we shall be partakers of His sufferings. Paul tells us in 2 Corinthians 1:5 that "The sufferings of Christ abound in us." The Apostle Paul longed to know "the fellowship of His sufferings" (Phil. 3:10). God allows testing and suffering in our lives that we may share with Him in His glory (Rom. 8:17). "Insofar as you are partakers of Christ's sufferings, rejoice," Peter tells us (1 Pet. 4:13). A sure promise is that "if we endure [*hupoménomen* {5278}, to abide under, endure, an exact synonym of *hupophérō*], we shall also reign with Him" (2 Tim. 2:12). Testings are minor in the lives of slothful Christians, but in the lives that God intends to use greatly, He sends great testings.

LESSONS:

1. Satan tempts us for the purpose of causing us to fail God.
2. God tests us to make us stronger and more useful.
3. We must never, as Christians, presume that we are standing securely, for when we do, we are surely on slippery ground.
4. God will not allow us to be tested beyond our human ability.
5. God is at all times trustworthy (1 Cor. 1:9).
6. No tests come upon the Christian without the Lord's permission.
7. Each test enables the believer to make progress in his Christian walk.
8. Each test provides the opportunity for victory.
9. God never liberates us from testing, but He gives us the joy of sharing in His glory.
10. The Lord promises endurance, not exemption from suffering and testing.
11. God deals with our **ability** to withstand the testing. We must deal with our **willingness**.

1 Cor. 10:14

Christians Must Flee from Idolatry

> *For this very reason, my beloved, flee far away from idolatry.*

In the beginning of chapter 10, Paul deals extensively with the problem of idolatry and its effect on believers. He then assures the Corinthian Christians that no temptation will come upon them that is beyond their ability to bear nor that is not common to man. Again now, Paul urges the Corinthians to be careful.

"For This Very Reason"

The word *dióper* (1355) is found in this verse and elsewhere in 1 Corinthians 8:13; 14:13. It derives from *diá* (1223), for; and the neuter relative pronoun *ho* from *hós* (3739), which, and *per* (4007), a particle expressing emphasis. We have elected to translate it "for this very reason." Let us not forget that the whole discussion of the Apostle Paul stems from whether or not a believer in Christ should be found participating with idolaters in their idol feasts. This would provide evidence not of how strong a believer is, as some must have claimed, but how arrogant he is by thinking he is beyond temptation and that he stands firmly (v. 12). If he decided to go into the idolater's banqueting feast, he would not likely stop with just eating meat, which in itself was not bad, but it is quite possible that he would be tempted into other practices of idolatry, such as fornication (see exegesis of the verb "play" under v. 7). It would be better not to go to such feasts at all than to go and presume upon the Lord's protection from such evil practices. The very atmosphere and temptation should be enough to keep one away. In 1 Corinthians 8:13, where the same expression *dióper* is used, Paul goes even farther in his cautious attitude and says that if simply eating meat may be associated with eating meat sacrificed to idols, he would rather not eat meat all his life than take the chance of becoming a stumbling block to his brother. He did not want to be considered as one who associated with idolatry.

"My Beloved"

To blunt the command's sharpness, Paul assures the Corinthian believers that, in spite of their faults, they are precious to him. He calls them "my beloved." While Paul cautions the Corinthian believers of the dangers that exist in finding themselves in the idol temples, he does not want to alienate them from himself. He wants to assure them that he is a loving brother to them, and that he does not want to see them treading on slippery ground, thinking that they stand securely. It is to be noted that the negative command is presented as a necessity. In 1 Corinthians 15:58, Paul gives the positive command when he says, "Therefore, my beloved brethren, be you steadfast [*hedraíoi*, the plural of *hedraíos* {1476}, from *hédra* (n.f.) which is a seat, chair, or base, thus meaning settled, steady, steadfast], unmovable, always abounding in the work of the Lord, forasmuch as you know that your labor is not in vain in the Lord." So in Paul's admonition, both the negative and the positive are necessary. It is advisable to tell the Corinthians that they must stand firmly, but it is also necessary to tell them how to avoid shaky ground. He clearly states that those who are found in the temple feasting with idolaters are placing themselves on unstable ground.

"Flee Far Away from Idolatry"

Whenever the Apostle Paul admonishes the Corinthian Christians to flee, he is not interested only in their temporary flight from idolatry and other sinful practices, but he is interested in their permanent avoidance of such temptations. He always says *pheúgete* (5343), you flee, which is the present imperative. Flee on a permanent basis, Paul urges the Corinthians, so that your character may not be tainted. For instance, in 1 Corinthians 6:18, he says, "Flee fornication"; and here in 10:14 he says, "Flee from idolatry." The two evils, idolatry and fornication, are closely associated. To young Timothy, Paul says, "But you, O man of God, flee [*pheúge*, the present singular active imperative] these things; and follow after righteousness, godliness, faith, love, patience, meekness" (1 Tim. 6:11). He refers to the sins he mentioned in the previous verses and also instructs Timothy to avoid covetous practices and the love of money. We find in 2 Timothy 2:22, that Paul tells him to "Flee [*pheúge*] also youthful lusts: but follow righteousness, faith, love, peace, with them that call on the Lord out of a pure heart." Timothy is urged to recognize that within him dwell lusts that he must constantly avoid.

Whereas in 1 Corinthians 6:18, 1 Timothy 6:11, and 2 Timothy 2:22, the verb has a direct object, here in the case of 1 Corinthians 10:14, the Apostle directs that we as Christians should distance ourselves as much as possible from idolatry. Any contact with idolatry is dangerous, not only direct contact such as participation in the feasts of idolatry, but also eating the meats sacrificed to idols. Whatever may give others the impression that we are soft on idolatry should be avoided, and it should be done on a consistent basis as a principle of our lives.

LESSONS:

1. Anything having to do with idolatry was of great concern to Paul who knew that the Corinthians lived in the midst of this temptation.
2. Paul does not hesitate to isolate the evil of idolatry and ask them to run away from it.
3. He realized that intimate contact with idolatry would cause one to be tainted by it, in spite of the fact that one could be victorious over it.
4. The Christians of Corinth are advised to completely disassociate themselves from idolatry and maintain their distance from it at all times.

1 Cor. 10:15

Judging Correctly about Meats Sacrificed to Idols

I speak assuming you to be sensible. You, yourselves, judge the rightness of what I am saying.

The Apostle Paul does not consider the Corinthians to be as stable and sensible as they should be. Otherwise, it would not be necessary for him to be writing these epistles of admonitions and warnings. They would be considered sensible if they judged correctly that which he is saying to them.

"I Speak Assuming You to Be Sensible"

"Assuming you" is a translation of the adverb *hōs* (5613), as. It is followed by *phronímois*, the dative plural of *phrónimos* (5429), heedful, sensible, practical when one deals with relationships with others. The word basically derives from *phrḗn* (5424) meaning the mind, and refers to the ability not only to think, but also to control one's thoughts and attitudes. The heart is the seat of passions, just as the mind is the seat of mental faculties. This is why in modern Greek *phrḗn* (used in the neuter plural, *phréna*) developed to mean "brake." Brakes help us to control an otherwise uncontrollable situation. When one can control himself properly in regard to the environment and his relationships to others, he is said to be *phrónimos*, prudent, sensible. The opposite of *phrónimos* is *áphrōn* (878), mindless, a fool. He is like a car

97

without brakes, and who knows where it will end up or what harm it will do?

Another antonym of *phrónimos* is *mōrós* (3474) meaning silly, stupid, foolish, from which we derive the English word "moron." In our Lord's parable of the ten virgins, we are told that five of them were sensible or prudent (*phrónimoi*) and five were foolish (*mōraí*, the feminine plural form of *mōrós* [Matt. 25:1–13]). The sensible ones thought of the future and considered the need to take oil in their vessels. The foolish ones, however, thought only of the present. Thus a fool can be characterized as one who thinks only of the present time without any consideration of the future.

In Matthew 7:24, our Lord illustrates a sensible man as one who does not build on shifting sand but on solid rock. It is much easier to build on sand, but it certainly is not permanent. The person who thinks only of the present and does not consider the eternal is a fool.

In Matthew 10:16, the Lord calls upon us to be wise like the serpents. Serpents are characterized by doing their work quietly and not boisterously.

In the parable of the faithful and sensible servant, in Matthew 24:45–51, the Lord considers that servant to be sensible who is responsible to accomplish his task even in the absence of his master. To believe that no one evaluates our work and that we are not accountable to anyone is certainly devoid of sense.

In the parable of the sensible steward in Luke 16:1–9, the Lord calls the man prudent who, during his lifetime thinks how he will be dealt with after his death.

There is the danger of considering ourselves to be sensible when in reality we are not (Rom. 11:25; 12:16). Our judgment concerning our wisdom should be based on the criteria that Christ sets for us (1 Cor. 4:10). The Apostle Paul does not tell the Corinthians that they are prudent or sensible. He says, "I speak **assuming** you to be sensible." In fact, they claimed that Paul was not prudent in how he elected to live and to sacrifice. He would not receive compensation for his work among them, he would not marry so that he could serve the Lord unhindered, and he preferred to lack in material things rather than to abound. This was foolish, according to the worldly standards of the Corinthians (2 Cor. 11:16–21). According to them, only a fool would deprive himself while he had the opportunity to enjoy the abundance of life. They could not understand such privation for the sake of Christ. Paul had ample reason to call the Corinthians babies, not spiritual but carnal (1 Cor. 3:1–3).

"You, Yourselves, Judge the Rightness of What I Am Saying"

Let us not forget that chapters 8 through 10 of 1 Corinthians is in answer to the question which the Corinthians put before Paul. This concerned meats sacrificed to idols and whether Christians should partake of them and sit at the idolater's feasts. Having given them some wise admonitions, he now assumes they can act as sensible people and judge what he is saying to them. The verb "I speak" is *légō* (3004), to speak. The Corinthians could not understand that there was a higher reason why Paul chose a life of sacrifice and suffering instead of a life of material abundance. It is as if Paul were saying to the Corinthians that there was a reason for everything he did and said, and Christ was that reason.

The second clause of our verse has a different verb for "I am saying." It is *phēmí* (5346), to say, meaning particularly to bring to light. By what is being said, Paul is appealing to the Corinthians' sense of understanding and comprehension. This is made clear by the use of the verb "judge" (*krínate*, the second person plural aorist active imperative of *krínō* [2919], to judge, to form an opinion after separating and considering the particulars of a case). This concerns the relationship between meat sacrificed to idols and three other practices. One is the practice of communion in the Christian church, referred to in verses 16 and 17. Another is that the practice of sacrifices offered to idols must be examined in relation to the sacrifices by Israel (v. 18). The third relationship is whether sacrifices to idols are sacrifices to nonentities or to demons (vv. 19, 20).

LESSONS:

1. Paul recognized that the Corinthians were lacking in spiritual judgment. He determined this from their behavior and actions (1 Cor. 3:1–3).
2. He assumed, however, that they should now begin to think as sensible Christians.
3. Paul indirectly supported his sacrificial life and conduct as being reasonable because of the Lord's mercy to him.
4. He challenged the Corinthians to understand what he was saying in regard to this whole matter of sacrifices to idols.

1 Cor. 10:16 | The Lord's Supper Is a Fellowship of Christ's Body

The cup of the blessing which we bless, is it not the fellowship of the blood of Christ? The bread which we break, is it not partaking of the body of Christ?

Many times in Scripture, physical objects are used symbolically. Thus, metonymically, the noun "cup" is used to represent its contents. The "cup," as referred to by Jesus Christ, represents His suffering on the cross. It was in the Garden of Gethsemane that our Lord prayed, "O My Father, if it be possible, let this cup [the neuter noun *potérion* {4221}, a drinking vessel, a cup, derived from *póō*, the ancient form of *pínō* {4095}, to drink] pass from Me: nevertheless, not as I will, but as Thou will" (Matt. 26:39). We must understand that this was not just any cup of suffering, but was one contrived by His enemies and given to Jesus by His heavenly Father. His death by crucifixion was imminent (Mark 14:36; Luke 22:42). In John 18:11, Jesus tells Peter that He did not need human defense in saving His life: "Then said Jesus unto Peter, 'Put up your sword into the sheath: the cup [*tópotérion*, meaning His death] which My Father has given Me, shall I not drink it?'" As Jesus said just after His betrayal, His Father who gave Him this cup to drink could presently give Him more than twelve legions of angels to rescue Him from death. However, His death was not only man's design, but was encompassed by the Father's eternal purpose. He endured the crucifixion so that Scripture would be fulfilled (Matt. 26:53, 54) and our souls might be saved.

Not only did God the Father give the Son the cup to drink, but also we find in the book of Acts that it was after the coming of the Holy Spirit that the practice of remembrance became a reality (1 Cor. 11:25). In Acts 2:1 the Holy Spirit came initiating the oneness of the church. In verse 41 we read, "Then they that gladly received His word were baptized: and the same day there were added unto them about three thousand souls." Verse 42 goes on to say, "And they continued steadfastly in the apostles' doctrine and fellowship, and in breaking of bread, and in prayers." It was God the Father, God the Son, and God the Holy Spirit who designed the salvation of man. The Father sent the Son who accepted the cup of death. When sinful men accept Jesus' substitutionary death, the Holy Spirit causes an immediate change, giving them the divine experience of a new birth and making them members of the body of Christ (1 Cor. 12:13). Believers are bound by the Holy Spirit, through faith in Jesus Christ, in the celebration of the death of Christ represented by the cup of suffering and crucifixion.

"The Cup of the Blessing"

The Apostle Paul chose to call Christ's death and crucifixion "the cup of blessing." Both words, "cup" and "blessing," have the definite article in front of them. The Greek text says "**the** cup of **the** blessing." Paul speaks of **the** cup of **the** blessing in 1 Corinthians 10:16, 17. This was the institution which came to be known in the Christian church as the Holy Eucharist. It is the commemoration of the work which Christ's shed blood has accomplished in the heart of the believer. The word "eucharist" is the rendering of *eucharistía* (2169) which means gratitude or thankfulness. The verb is *eucharistéō* (2168), to be grateful or to give thanks. Thus, the Lord's Supper is the institution of thanksgiving, because we read in Matthew 26:27; Mark 14:23, and Luke 22:17 that our Lord, during the night He was betrayed, took the cup, and after He gave thanks, He gave to His disciples to drink of the fruit of the vine. This feast of the Christian church then came to be known as the "Feast of the Eucharist," the thanksgiving.

It behooves us to analyze the words *eucharistía*, thanksgiving, and the verb *eucharistéō*. They are derived from *eú* (2095), meaning good or well, and the noun *cháris* (5485), grace, particularly that which causes joy, pleasure, gratification, favor, and acceptance. *Cháris* refers to the grace of God which changes individuals when they accept with thanksgiving what Christ has done in their hearts. The person who is changed in this manner and born again (John 3) is full of gratitude. Therefore, the Feast of the Holy Eucharist is a feast which gives Christians the opportunity to express their gratitude to God and their satisfaction for what He, through His grace, has done in their hearts and lives. It is not a feast for unbelievers, but for those who believe and have appropriated the grace of God.

That the cup does not contain the actual blood of Christ is obvious. The Lord instituted this feast of gratitude before His blood was shed. He said that it was the blood of the New Testament in order to distinguish it from the blood of the Old Testament in which animals were sacrificed (Luke 22:20). The New Testament is called *hē* (the) *Kainḗ* (New) *Diathḗkē* (Testament or Covenant). Note that this is referred to as **the** New Testament, as contrasted to the Old Testament by the same Apostle in 2 Corinthians 3:14. *Kainḗ* (new) is the feminine of *kainós* (2537), qualitatively new, and not only chronologically recent which would have been expressed by the adjective *néa*, the feminine of *néos* (3501), new. Paul makes the qualitatively new New Testament stand in contrast to the Old (*palaiá*, the feminine of *palaiós* [3820], old, meaning previous, but not first which would have been expressed by *archaía*, the feminine of *archaíos* {744}, original) Testament. The original testament or dispensation was that of innocence. When God created man, He did not create a sinful being, but one with whom He could have fellowship. However, as we know, man fell from his original state and became a sinful human being, separated from the fellowship of the Holy God (Gen. 3:13). Thus man, from the time of his fall until the coming of Christ, lived in the Old Testament dispensation in which men sacrificed animals in seeking forgiveness for their sins (Heb. 9:6–9). In the New Testament we do not sacrifice animals anymore because the sacrifice of Christ was once and for all for the sins of the world (Heb. 9:26–28).

This perfect, completed, and enduring sacrifice of Jesus Christ is for the cancellation (*athétēsis* [115], cancellation, disannulling, abolition) of sin (Heb. 9:26). The blood of Jesus Christ accomplished what the blood of animals could not accomplish. The acceptance of that sacrifice by faith causes the believer to be saved, and in his heart there is born unspeakable thanksgiving and blessing. Grace (*cháris*) can then be taken as the equivalent of *eulogía* (2129), blessing. The word *eulogía* derives from *eú*, well, good, and the verb *légō* (3004), to speak. Therefore, blessing means to speak well of or to wish well. The shedding of the blood of Christ was for the benevolence of man. That is why it is called "**the** cup of **the** blessing." It reminds us of how God intervened on our behalf. Only those who recognize their need and appropriate the blood of Christ through faith (Eph. 2:8) receive the blessing intended for man. The shedding of the blood of Christ does not automatically cleanse a person from sin until he acknowledges that he is sinful and needs the sacrifice of God's Son on his behalf. The benefit of this blessing comes by faith and it results in the creation of a new person (2 Cor. 5:17).

Thus, the blood of Christ becomes the cup of the blessing to any individual who accepts by faith the substitutionary death of Christ.

"Which We Bless"

This cup of blessing, which we bless, becomes the joining force of all believers. The verb is *eulogoúmen*, the first person plural present active indicative of *eulogéō* (2127), to bless, speak well of. In what way do we speak well of the cup of blessing which represents the blood that Christ shed on the cross for the remission of our sins? This blessing is given by believers who are members of the Church or the body of Jesus Christ (Eph. 1:22, 23) in their active remembrance of the sacrifice of Christ on their behalf. "We bless" does not mean that we add to it, but that we recognize it as having been done for our benevolence, our spiritual well-being. The verb *eulogéō* is equivalent to *eucharistéō* which means to thank or be grateful for (Matt. 26:26; Mark 14:22; Luke 24:30). Therefore, the celebration of the Lord's Supper ought to be a time of special remembrance and thanksgiving for the blood of the Lord Jesus Christ (Eph. 1:7; Heb. 9:22; 10:11, 18).

"Is It Not the Fellowship of the Blood of Christ?"

Those who have been washed by the blood of Christ (Rev. 1:5) constitute a fellowship (*koinōnía* [2842], fellowship with, participation; see Acts 2:42; 1 Cor. 1:9; 10:16 [twice]; 2 Cor. 6:14; 8:4; 13:13; Gal. 2:9; Eph. 3:9; Phil. 1:5). The word *koinōnía* means to have something in common, from the verb *koinóō* (2840), to make common, and the adjective *koinós* (2839), common. When we partake of one cup, we show that we have in common the forgiveness of our sins made possible through the shed blood of the Lord Jesus Christ. Those who have not experienced forgiveness by grace through faith (Eph. 2:8), no matter how many times they partake of communion, cannot comprehend its true meaning. We must be careful that we never convey to the sinful individual the idea that he will experience regeneration by partaking of the Lord's Supper.

To make sure that the word *koinōnía*, fellowship or participation, is understood, Paul does not say, "they who participate of the same physical cup of the fruit of the vine," but rather he speaks of the participation of the blood of Christ. This fellowship consists of people who have, by faith, appropriated the blood of Christ as the cleansing agent for their hearts and who have received forgiveness of sin, having been joined together with Christ.

Notice that Paul does not say "the blood of Jesus," but "the blood of Christ [the Anointed One]." It refers to the blood of the Son of God, and not of the man Jesus only. It was not mere human blood that was shed which has joined us together in a common brotherhood with the experience of sins forgiven, but it was the blood of Christ, the eternal Messiah, the Son of God, who forever had been with the Father (John 1:18). It does not say "the wine" or "the fruit of the vine" that joins us to Jesus Christ (1 Cor. 12:13) and to one another as children of God (John 1:12). It is the blood of Christ, and not just the representative element which cleanses us from all sin (1 John 1:7).

The "not" in the phrase "is it not" is the Greek adverb *ouchí* (3780) from the absolute negative *ou* (3756), not. This adverb in negative questions implies an affirmative answer as in Matthew 5:46; 20:13; Luke 12:6; 17:8, 17; John 11:9, and Romans 3:29. Every time believers gather to celebrate Holy Communion, they declare as a body that they have first become members of the spiritual body of Christ through His atoning blood. They are joined together with Him and with one another through their common faith in Christ, and it is all due to the sacrifice of the Lamb of God.

"The Bread Which We Break, Is It Not Partaking of the Body of Christ?"

Then Paul asks a second negative question which necessitates an affirmative answer as in the previous sentence: "The bread which we break, is it not [*ouchí*, the absolute 'not'] partaking of the body of Christ?" The word which we translated "partaking" is the same word as in the previous sentence, *koinōnía*, but for the sake of clarity of meaning, we have elected to translate it as "partaking" instead of "fellowship." As "the cup" is one cup, so "the body" is one body (*sōma* [4983]) of Christ. There is only one cup, one blood, and one body. This is the physical body of Christ, in which flowed the physical blood of the Son of man. As the physical blood was shed for us by Christ, so was His body broken for us.

It is to be noted that both verbs, *eulogoúmen*, we bless, and *kláomen or klōmen*, the first person plural present active indicative of *kláō* (2806), we break, are in the present active indicative form. This means that the believer partaking of the Lord's Supper has blessed or thanked the Lord for his individual partaking of the cup, and has broken for himself a piece from the bread that served all the believers assembled in one place. The participation in the Lord's Supper always involved the breaking of an individual piece from the loaf (Luke 24:35; Acts 2:42). This was known as the *klásis* (2800), the breaking of the bread, from the verb *kláō*, to break. The fact that the two verbs are in the active indicative implies the individual responsibility that each assumes when partaking of the cup and the bread. It is possible that an individual may partake of the Lord's Supper unworthily (*anaxíōs* [371], unworthily, irreverently, in an unbecoming manner), treating the Lord's Supper as a common meal, without attributing to it and its elements their proper value (1 Cor. 11:27, 29). When the Lord instituted this Holy Supper and gave the elements to His disciples, He did not exclude Judas, for we read that "they all drank of it" (Mark 14:23). The Lord knew that Judas was not a true disciple, but yet He did not exclude him from participation. Judas himself bore the responsibility of unworthily partaking of the elements of the Lord's Supper.

LESSONS:

1. The Lord's Supper is called by Paul "the cup of the blessing."
2. Only those who have allowed the blood of Christ to cleanse them from sin should participate in this cup.
3. The communion does not benefit an unbeliever who partakes of it.
4. An unbeliever who partakes of it is said to partake "unworthily" (1 Cor. 11:27, 29).
5. The bread and the cup symbolize the broken body and shed blood of Christ. Each person who partakes of these elements bears individual responsibility for so doing.
6. The mere participation in the cup and the bread reconciles an individual to God, because only those who are already reconciled can partake of it worthily.
7. The cup of blessing and the bread which we break are the symbols of a memorial feast which bring vividly into the heart of the believer God's sacrifice to redeem him from sin (1 Cor. 11:24).

1 Cor. 10:17 | *Believers Constitute the Body of Christ*

Because there is one bread, we who are many are one body, for we all partake of one bread.

In the Corinthian church there was a tendency to divisiveness: "Now this I say, that every one of you says, I am of Paul; and I of Apollos; and I of Cephas; and I of Christ. Is Christ divided? Was Paul crucified for you? Or were you baptized in the name of Paul?" (1 Cor. 1:12, 13). When Christians meet to celebrate the Lord's Supper, they should have one unifying thought—that they all belong to Christ. It is important to remember our unity in Him and with one another when we take the Lord's Supper. This is the reason Paul gives the advice in 1 Corinthians 11:28, 29: "Let a man examine himself, and so let him eat of that bread, and drink of that cup. For he that eats and drinks unworthily, eats and drinks damnation to himself, not discerning the Lord's body." Although this has definite reference to unbelievers, it includes believers who may have resentment in their hearts toward other believers. If they partake of the Lord's Supper with any malice or bitterness that separates them from their brothers in Christ, they are eating of the bread unworthily. The oneness of the bread is symbolic of the unity of believers who constitute the body of Christ (Rom. 12:5; 1 Cor. 12:13, 27; Eph. 1:23; 2:16; 4:4, 12, 16; 5:23, 30; Col. 1:18, 24; 2:19; 3:15).

"Because There Is One Bread"

This verse explains what the word *koinōnía* (2842), fellowship or participation, of the previous verse means. The conjunction *hóti* (3754), because, concerning that, with which this verse begins must be viewed as a connector tying this verse together with the previous one. It could be translated "because [seeing that] we who are many, are one." It stresses the unity of believers in the Person of Jesus Christ. It asserts what Paul says in 1 Corinthians 12:13 that "by one Spirit we are all baptized into one body, whether we be Jews or Gentiles, whether we be bond or free; and have been all made to drink into one Spirit."

"We Who Are Many Are One Body"

As believers united in Christ, we do not lose our individual identity. This is why Paul adds, "We who are many are one body." We are individuals who have the nature of God within us (2 Pet. 1:4). When we become children of God, we do not lose our individual identity, but we acquire the spiritual nature which is common to all believers. We should never allow any particular idiosyncrasy to hide the nature of God which indwells us. That which distinguishes us as individuals should never be more prominent than that which unites us as children of God in Jesus Christ.

"For We All Partake of One Bread"

A vivid reminder of our unity in Christ is the fact that we all partake (*metéchomen*, the first person plural present active indicative of *metéchō* [3348], to partake of, participate in, derived from *metá* [3326], with, denoting association, and *échō* [2192], have) of the same loaf. The verb *metéchō* then means to have an association with another. This verb is usually used with the genitive form of something in which one participates (1 Cor. 9:12; 10:21). "For we all partake of one bread" is the only occasion where the verb is used with the preposition *ek* (1537), out of. It speaks of our derivation, that we are all born out of Christ. However, it does not mean that by participating in communion we become members of the body of Christ. This also definitely indicates that only those who have been born of Christ should partake of the bread. It also indicates that it is only through Christ that we can be saved. Peter says in Acts 4:12, "Neither is there salvation in any other: for there is none other name under heaven [that is, Christ, the Bread of Life] given among men, whereby we must be saved." In 1 Corinthians 11:28, Paul says, "But let a man examine himself, and so let him eat [*ek* {1537}, out of] of that bread, and drink of [*ek*] that cup." It is the explicit teaching of the Word of God that he who is not of Christ should not participate in the breaking of the bread.

LESSONS:

1. The Lord's Supper should always be an occasion for remembering the unity of the body of Christ.
2. It should also be an occasion for self-examination.
3. Having the nature of God in us does not make us all the same, but the characteristics of the nature of God should predominate.
4. We can, as believers, have individual characteristics, but must never allow them to blot out our common characteristics as believers.
5. Only those who are of Christ ought to participate in the celebration of the unity of Christ.

1 Cor. 10:18

Consider the Israelites!

Consider Israel according to the flesh; are not they which eat of the sacrifices partakers of the altar?

Paul writes as an Israelite to Israelites, for he himself was one who became a Christian when the Lord's unique call was given directly to him after Christ's resurrection (Acts 9:1–9; 22:6–16; 26:12–18). The name "Israel" referred to the Jews who were born into the Jewish religion. In the New Testament, this term is applied to all the descendants of Israel which was originally a name indicating special privilege given by God to Jacob, a great ancestor of the race (Gen. 32:28; 35:10). The name "Israel" differs from "Hebrew" which, in New Testament times at least, stood for Jews of purely national sympathies who spoke the Hebrew or Aramaic dialect (Acts 6:1). The term "Jew," on the other hand, was originally applied to all who belonged to the promised Judah and, after the Babylonian captivity, to all of the ancient race wherever located. Those known as Israel, therefore, are pre-eminently a people of privilege, having been chosen by God and having received His covenant. Thus the Jewish orator Paul frequently addressed the people as "men of Israel" (Acts 2:22; 3:12; 4:8 [elders of Israel], 10 [people of Israel]; 5:35; 13:16).

In the Acts of the Apostles we find the word "Israel" used historically with reference to the ancestors of the Jews of apostolic times, and to the Jews generally. The history of Israel, as God's chosen people, is referred to in the speeches contained in the Book of Acts, for example, by Steven (7:23, 37, 42) and by Paul (13:17; 28:20). It is usually assumed or suggested in Acts that the Jews to whom the gospel was being preached were the Israelites, the people for whom God had special favor and who might expect special blessings (5:31; 13:23). Later, the term "Israel" acquired a spiritual significance and was used metaphorically. This was due to the rejection of the gospel by the nation of Israel.

"Consider Israel According to the Flesh"

Here we find Paul differentiating between the natural descendants of the nation of Israel and the spiritual descendants who are called the true Israel of God (Rom. 9:6). He refers to the natural descendants as "Israel after the flesh," or those who belong to the "stock of Israel" (Phil. 3:5). On the other hand, he speaks of a "commonwealth of Israel" (Eph. 2:12) or "Israel of God" (Gal. 6:16), from which all men, even Jews by birth, are aliens, but into which the Ephesians had been admitted (Eph. 2:13). By this "commonwealth of Israel" or "Israel of God," the Apostle refers to the true, spiritual Israel, practically equivalent to all the faithful. It might be defined as the whole number of the elect who have been, are, or shall be gathered into one entity under Christ.

This true Israel does not necessarily coincide with the nation or the stock of Abraham. "They are not all Israel, which are of Israel" (Rom. 9:6), that is, by racial descent. Paul thus distinguishes the Jews who did not accept the gospel, who were merely descendants of Israel, as "Israel according to the flesh." This Israel adhered to Jewish traditions without being a true spiritual Israel.

"Are Not They Which Eat of the Sacrifices Partakers of the Altar?"

A descendant of Israel ate of the sacrifices of the temple, and by thus eating, he was confirming his racial descent. By so doing, he expressed agreement with the whole system.

The word translated "partakers" is the adjectival noun *koinōnós* (2844) which relates to the noun *koinōnía* (2842), fellowship or partnership, twice used in verse 16. Christians participating in the Lord's Supper partake of the cup and the bread to affirm their relationship with Jesus Christ and His death and resurrection and coming again (1 Cor. 11:26). As the symbolic act of partaking of the fruit of the vine and the bread is a confirmation of what they represent to the believer, just as the partaking of the sacrificed meat for the "Israelites according to the flesh" was an association with and acceptance of the traditional meaning of the altar in the temple, and this is what Paul wants us to consider (*blépete*, the second person plural present active imperative of *blépō* [991], to heed, see, consider). This illustration that Paul brings from the ceremonial tradition of the Jews confirms his teaching that one does not become a Christian by partaking of the cup and the bread, but contrariwise, he partakes because he is a Christian.

To the rhetorical question, "Are not they which eat of the sacrifices partakers of the altar?" the expected answer is an affirmative yes. It follows the pattern which Paul uses in verse 16, "Is it not the fellowship of Christ's blood?" and, of course, the answer is yes. The English "not" is the Greek adverb *ouchí* (3780) from the absolute negative *ou* (3756) which, in negative questions, implies an affirmative answer. Paul is asking the question in order to stress that they who eat sacrificed animals are participating in the whole process. They should not be merely consuming meat without realizing what they are doing. "The sacrifices [*tás*, the accusative plural feminine of the article *ho* {3588}, the; *thusías*, the accusative plural feminine of the noun *thusía* {2378}, sacrifice]" referred to meats offered as sacrifices according to the Levitical system. Part of the sacrifice was burned on the altar and part was given to the priests (Mark 9:49, cf. Lev. 7:13, 33; Luke 13:1; Acts 7:41; see Lev. chs. 2, 3). Here in 1 Corinthians 10:18, the sentence means "those who eat the victims [or animals] sacrificed," which was done by the priests and persons offering the sacrifices (Sept.: Ex. 34:15; Lev. 8:31; Deut. 12:6, 7, 27). These were Jews who by descent became partakers (*koinōnoí*, the plural of *koinōnós*, partaker) of the Jewish altar. This was called the *thusiastḗrion* (2379), an altar of the true God (see Matt. 5:23, 24; 23:18–20; Rom. 11:3; Heb. 7:13; James 2:21; Sept.: Gen. 8:20; 12:7) and referred specifically to the altar for burnt offerings in the temple (Matt. 23:35; Luke 11:51; 1 Cor. 9:13; 10:18; Heb. 13:10). The altar, however, used by the heathen or the non-Jews in sacrifice to their idols, is called *bōmós*. (1041), an idol altar. The only place the words "idol altar" is found in the New Testament is in Acts 17:23 in Paul's speech to the heathen Athenians.

The argument of the Apostle Paul is that the Christian who participates in the Lord's Supper partakes of the body of Christ knowing that His body was sacrificed on the cross and that His blood was shed in order to reconcile man to God (2 Cor. 5:14, 15, 17; 1 Pet. 1:19). In 1 Corinthians 5:7, Paul says, "For even Christ our Passover is sacrificed for us." The Christian believer must not partake lightly of the Lord's Supper without due consideration of its significant meaning. To those who have not experienced reconciliation with God, participation in the Lord's Supper is meaningless, and the person does not attribute the proper value to the meal. Those participating in this way are said to participate "unworthily" (1 Cor. 11:27, 29). In the same way, the Jews who ate the animals sacrificed on the

Jewish altar were to be conscious that the blood of the sacrifices was shed to cover their sin or they were eating sacrifices unworthily.

LESSONS:

1. The word "Israel" can be used to mean "Israel according to the flesh" who belonged to the "stock of Israel" (Phil. 3:5), and the "commonwealth of Israel" (Eph. 2:12). It can also mean the "Israel of God" (Gal. 6:16) from which many, even Jews by birth, are aliens.
2. The "Israel of God" (Gal. 6:16) is the true, spiritual Israel to whom belong all the faithful.
3. As both "Israel in the flesh" and the true "Israel of God" participated in the eating of the animals sacrificed on the altar, likewise both believers and unbelievers participate in the Lord's Supper. The first do it worthily by virtue of being born again into Christ, whereas the second do it unworthily by virtue of merely participating in the Christian system.

1 Cor. 10:19

Idols and Sacrifices to Them Are Nothing

What then am I saying? That the idol is something?
Or that meat sacrificed to idols is something?

A problem arose in Corinth because some believers considered it permissible and consistent with their Christian testimony to partake of meats sacrificed to idols. The main subject of chapters 8, 9, and 10 of 1 Corinthians is that of "things sacrificed to idols" (1 Cor. 8:1).

Paul teaches that the memorial feast of Holy Communion is a celebration of a real occurrence. Jesus Christ came into the world, shed His blood on the cross, and died so that He could save sinners (1 Tim. 1:15). History attests to this fact. Not only did He die, but He rose again. Paul proves this occurrence in 1 Corinthians 15. This was not a chance event, but as Peter said in his Pentecostal address in Acts 2:22, "You men of Israel, hear these words; Jesus of Nazareth, a man approved [*apodedeigménon*, the accusative singular masculine perfect passive participle of *apodeíkneimi* {584}, to demonstrate, prove] of God among you by miracles and wonders and signs, which God did by Him in the midst of you, as you yourselves also know." Jesus Christ, a historical figure, was not a personality of chance, but the One who was sent by the Father to make known to mankind the real God (John 1:18). As 1 John 5:20 affirms,

We perceive, nevertheless, that the Son of God is come [*hēkei*, the third person singular present active indicative of *hēko* {2240}, to come, with the emphasis of being here], and has given [*dédōken*, the third person singular perfect active indicative of *dídōmi* {1325}, to give as a gift] us intelligence [*diánoian*, the accusative form of *diánoia* {1271}, intelligence, understanding, intellectual faculty], so that we know experientially [*ginóskōmen*, the first person plural present active subjunctive of *ginoáskō* {1097}, to know experientially, referring to that initial realization and acceptance] the true One [*alēthinón*, the accusative singular masculine adjectival form of *alēthinós* {228}, which refers to God versus the false gods who have no reality], and we are in the true One, in His Son Jesus Christ. This One is the true God and the eternal life (a.t.).

If it were not for Jesus Christ, we would not know the true God from the false gods. Therefore, the first argument that Paul brings in presenting the Christian remembrance of Jesus Christ, His death, His resurrection, and His coming again (1 Cor. 11:26) is to prove to the Corinthians that the God whom Jesus Christ revealed is the true God. He is not another false god of the heathen, nor is He first among equals because the others are false gods. Rather, He is the only true God.

The second argument Paul presents is that the God in whom Israel believed, even the "Israel after the flesh," is the same God whom Jesus Christ later revealed (v. 18). The sacrifices that Israel made were not sacrifices to a false god, but to the real God who dwelt in the Holy of Holies, into which the high priest entered once a year to sacrifice animals for the sins of himself and other people. This was a foreshadowing of Jesus Christ who died once and for all for the sins of the world (Heb. 7:26–28; 9:11, 12). The reality, then, of the God of the Jews was confirmed by the same Person, Jesus Christ of history.

"What Then Am I Saying?"

When Paul asks the question, "What then am I saying?" he is referring back to verses 16 to 18. He declares that the celebration of the death, resurrection, and coming again of Jesus Christ confirms that He was the Son of God who came to explain Deity.

"That an Idol Is Something? Or That Meat Sacrificed to Idols Is Something?"

Paul is not reversing himself and telling us something contrary to 1 Corinthians 8:4, 5 that an idol is nothing in the world. All idols are mere figments of man's imagination, but there is only one true God who is real. Paul defends his comments in those verses by saying that if idols are nothing, so are sacrifices to idols. He then adds, "Or that meat sacrificed to idols is something?" If the idol is nothing, then whatever is sacrificed to it has no real meaning.

The answers to these questions that Paul poses is an emphatic No! There is only one true God whom Jesus came to reveal explicitly (*exēgésato*, the third person singular aorist middle deponent indicative of *exēgéomai* [1834], to explicitly reveal, explain, bring out of the hiding place). Jesus Christ has declared Him to us that we might believe and have eternal life (John 1:18; see author's book *Was Christ God?*).

LESSONS:

1. Paul here contrasts reality with unreality.
2. He confirms the fact that idols have no reality and, therefore, meat sacrificed to idols has no real significance as he stated in 1 Corinthians 8:4, 5.
3. The contrast, however, is with the reality of the true God whom Jesus Christ came to reveal, the same God of the Israelites unto whom meaningful sacrifices were made, as confirmed by the substitutionary death and resurrection of Jesus Christ.

1 Cor. 10:20 | *Heathen Sacrifices Are in Reality Made to Demons*

But what the heathen sacrifice, they sacrifice to demons and absolutely not to God. By no means do I want you to become partakers of the demons.

Corinth and Athens were heathen cities (Acts 17:16). The Jews came to Corinth from Italy (Acts 18:2) and constituted a religious minority of that great metropolitan city. The Gentiles or the heathen (*tá éthnē*, the nominative plural neuter of *éthnos* [1484], nations, meaning Gentile nations, those other than the Jewish nation, hence heathen, idolaters) constituted the majority of the population of Corinth.

"But What the Heathen Sacrifice, They Sacrifice to Demons"

In their worship, the Gentiles sacrificed animals to idols. "Sacrifice" is the translation of the verb *thúei*, the third person singular present active indicative of *thúō* (2380), to kill and offer in sacrifice. The altar, however, which they used, was neither called *thusiastērion* (2379), which was what the Jews called their altar, nor the altar of the true God. Rather, it was called *bōmós* (1041), the idolater's altar (Acts 17:23). By the word "what" (*há*, the accusative plural neuter form of the relative pronoun *hós* [3739]) Paul is referring to the animals sacrificed. The difference, however, between the Jews and the heathen is that the Jews sacrificed

123

to the true God, as prescribed to them in the Old Testament, whereas the heathen sacrificed to demons.

The Apostle Paul declares that the heathen gods are demons (*daimónia*). First Corinthians 10:20, 21 is the only passage in the Corinthian epistles in which Paul mentions demons. Those things which the heathen sacrificed, they sacrificed to demons (*daimoníois*, the dative plural neuter form of the noun *daimónion* [1140] little demon, the diminutive of *daímōn* [1142]), for they were feared greatly. The word *daímōn* occurs only five times (Matt. 8:31; Mark 5:12; Luke 8:29; Rev. 16:14; 18:2), but *daimónion* is used many times. They are also called unclean spirits (Luke 4:33; 8:29, etc.); an evil spirit (Luke 7:21; 8:2); a dumb (mute or unable to speak) spirit (Mark 9:17); a spirit of infirmity (Luke 13:11), and a spirit of divination (*púthōnos*, the genitive of *púthōn* [4436], the Greek name given to the mythological serpent or dragon which lived at Pytho, beneath Mount Parnassus, and guarded the Delphic Oracle; Acts 16:16). Demons, then, are spirits which oppose the kingdom of God.

When Paul visited Athens and addressed the Athenians on Mars Hill, he said, "I perceive that in all things you are too superstitious" (Acts 17:22). In verse 16 we find that his spirit was vexed because he found the city full of idols (*katheídōlon* [2712]). The word that is translated "superstitious" is the Greek word *deisidaimonestérous* (1174) which is the comparative degree of *deisidaímōn*, fear of gods, superstitious. It is derived from the verb *deidō* (n.f.), to fear, and *daímōn*, demon. Paul found the Athenians extremely fearful of evil spirits, and, in order to pacify these spirits, they built idols to worship them. The demons, then, to whom the heathen sacrificed, were in total contrast to the God of the Christians. They were evil and vindictive spirits, while the God of the Bible, whom Christ came to reveal, is not vicious, but loving (1 John 4:8, 16). The key verse of the New Testament is John 3:16, "For God so loved the world. . . ." The sacrifices of the Old Testament were for the purpose of atoning for man's sin, and were an example or prophecy of what Christ would do for the sin of the world (Heb. 9:28; 10:4). The Old Testament sacrifices were not at all enough to reconcile men to God. That system was merely the shadow of a better one to come.

When Paul stated that the heathen sacrificed to the demons, he may have had in mind the exact wording of the Septuagint of Deuteronomy 32:17, "They sacrificed to devils, and not to God." Psalm 96:5 tells us, "For all the gods of the nations are idols: but the Lord made the heavens."

How do we reconcile 1 Corinthians 8:4 where Paul asserts that an idol is nothing, that is to say, not a real being, while here he associates idols with demons? The fact that Paul mentions the names attributed to temples, such as the Temple of Apollo and the Temple of Artemis, does not mean that Apollo and Artemis or other Greek mythological gods were real personalities. All that he tells us in this verse is that sacrifices made to idols were connected with the demon world, that is, the satanic world. It is interesting, indeed, that the word "demons" in the epistles is always used in the plural. No identity is given to them because they represent the powers of evil, with their head being Satan. While the heathen consider their idols to be their gods, in actuality they are not gods, but unidentifiable demons.

"And *Absolutely* Not to God"

Observe, however, that in contrast to the demons, Paul says, "And not to God." The "not" is the absolute negative *ou* (3756). This is why we have translated it as "absolutely not." The word "God" does not have the definite article in front of it which implies that Paul is referring to the true God or the Godhead in three Persons, God the Father, God the Son, and God the Holy Spirit. (See author's book entitled *Was Christ God?* and particularly the examination of the word "God" in John 1:18, with which the verse begins in Greek.)

"By No Means Do I Want You to Become Partakers of the Demons"

Paul asserts that he who has fellowship with idols has fellowship with the demons in which idolatry finds its expression. Paul speaks in no uncertain terms when he says, "By no means do I want you to become partakers of the demons." Again, he uses the absolute "not" (*ou*). The verb *thélō* (2309) expresses not only desire, but executive will, active volition and purpose. He did not want, by any means, the Christians to be partakers (*koinōnoús*, the adjectival noun of the substantive *koinōnía* [2842], participation, fellowship) of demon worship which they certainly are when they partake of the idol feasts. The Christian believer should flee from such things (1 Cor. 10:14). The word "to become" is *gínesthai*, the present middle/passive deponent infinitive of *gínomai* (1096), to become, which is a far better rendering than simply "to be."

LESSONS:

1. Idol worship is definitely related to Satan and demon worship.
2. Idol sacrifices have nothing to do with the real God of Israel and the sacrifices of the Old Testament for the sins of the people, nor have they any equivalence to the sacrifice of Christ for the remission of sins.
3. Demons belong to the kingdom of Satan, and Christians ought to have nothing to do with them.

1 Cor. 10:21 | *Idolatry Cannot Be Practiced with Christianity*

You absolutely cannot be drinking the cup of the Lord and the cup of demons. You absolutely cannot be partaking of the Lord's table and of the table of demons.

In verse 20, Paul tells the Corinthians that he absolutely does not want them to participate in idol feasts. He expresses this by the absolute negative *ou* (3756). Now here in verse 21, he states an impossibility which exists because of the nature of the things involved. There are substances that naturally do not mix. Oil, for instance, does not blend with water. As there are things that do not mix physically, so there are spiritual things that, by the nature of their being, cannot be mixed. Among these are idolatry and Christianity. As Paul stated in the previous verse, it is not because idols are realities (1 Cor. 8:4), but because they represent the demon world. On the other hand, Christians, in their practice, represent the true and real God in three Persons as revealed by Christ, and this real God does not have anything in common with idolatry.

But you ask, has not God created everything, including the demons? Yes, God did create everything in its original form and state. God created angels in the spiritual world to minister to people. The demons, together with their leader, Satan, were angels before they chose to disobey God. Their whole story is summarized succinctly in Jude 6: "And the angels which kept not their first estate, but left their own habitation, He has reserved in everlasting chains under darkness unto the judgment of the great day." The verb "left" means to leave behind of their own volition (*apolipóntas*, the accusative plural masculine second aorist active of the participle *apoleípō* [620], to leave voluntarily, derived from the preposition *apó* [575], from, and *leípō* [3007], to be absent or lack). The Lord said to His disciples, "I beheld Satan as lightning fall from heaven" (Luke 10:18). The demons, therefore, are fallen angels who are awaiting their day of judgment. They are spiritual beings who continue their destructive work, deceiving people into thinking that they are worshiping the true God, while indeed they are worshiping the demons.

"You Absolutely Cannot Be Drinking the Cup of the Lord and the Cup of Demons"

How can two antithetical spiritual forces sit in fellowship together? With this Paul is saying that you cannot (*ou*, the absolute "not"; *dúnasthe*, the second person plural present middle/passive deponent form of *dúnamai* [1410], to be able, can), by the nature of the Lord's cup, keep drinking it and, at the same time, keep drinking the cup of demons. The infinitive "to drink" is *pínein*, the present active infinitive of *pínō* (4095), to drink, which indicates habitual drinking. Paul is not speaking of the newly converted Christian who may have sat once or twice at the heathen table, but of one who has made it a practice to go to both the communion service and the table of demons. Furthermore, he does not refer to one who simply attends without participating, because he says, "You cannot be drinking the cup of the Lord and the cup of demons." This individual is not merely a spectator, he is a participant. Paul is referring to the born-again Christian who knows what he is doing when he drinks the cup that represents Christ's blood and when he eats the bread that represents the body of Christ on the cross. Such a born-again believer, partaking of the communion service, cannot also partake on a consistent, regular basis, of the cup of demons. No one can worship both the true God and demons. Demons are rebellious, spiritual beings who are waiting for their day of judgment.

"You Absolutely Cannot Be Partaking of the Lord's Table and of the Table of Demons"

Paul moves from the drinking of the cup to participation in the table of the Lord and the table of demons. The difference between the cup and the table is that the cup represents the actual drinking and eating of the elements, whereas the table represents partaking in the whole celebration. The communion service, for instance, would include singing and worship of the Lord Jesus and the expression of His love.

Again, the verb here is in the infinitive, *metéchein*, the present active infinitive of *metéchō* (3348), to partake, which is derived from *metá* (3326), with, denoting association, and *échō* (2192), have. This verb implies that the word *pínein*, drink, includes participation in all that the demons stand for when one takes part in the total feast of idolatry. Idol feasts were gluttonous, drunken, sexual orgies which are repugnant to a child of God.

Paul wants us to understand that when we participate in the communion service, we participate in all that it stands for, including our oneness with other participants. On the other hand, when we participate in the feast of idolatry, we make ourselves one with idolaters and their evils. This is impossible for a Christian to do consciously.

LESSONS:

1. It is a spiritual absolute that Christianity and idolatry do not mix.

2. Christianity and idolatry do not mix because one is inspired by Christ who is God, the Second Person of the Trinity, and the other is inspired by demons who are opposed to Christ.

3. Demons were not created as such, but were created as angels who voluntarily left heaven and incurred the first judgment of God in their separation from Him and in their becoming disturbing forces of darkness.

4. Satan and his cohorts are not always going to continue their evil pursuits, for their final judgment is certain (Rev. 20:10).

1 Cor. 10:22

Rejection Brings God's Wrath

Or shall we continue to provoke the Lord to jealousy? Are we inherently stronger than He is?

Can one be a Christian and at the same time be an idolater? Can one add Christ as a god to his pantheon of idols in an idolatrous practice? The answer is an emphatic No! The true God has been revealed (1 John 5:20) by the unique (*monogenēs* [3439]) Son, who was virgin born (Matt. 1:10-23), miracle working, and who died and resurrected Himself the third day (Matt. 16:21; Mark 16:7, 8).

"Or Shall We Continue to Provoke the Lord to Jealousy?"

This verse begins with the disjunctive particle *ē* (2228), "or," which remains untranslated in the King James Version, the Revised Standard Version, the New International Version, and others, but is rendered as "or" in the New American Standard Version. It shows the alternative to the acceptable attitude toward the only true God. Paul expresses this in view of the duration of idolatry among some who thought they could participate in the Lord's Supper and, at the same time, in the feasts of idol temples.

The verb that the Apostle Paul is using is *parazēloúmen*, the first person plural present active indicative of *parazēlóō*

(3863) from *pará* (3844), to the point of, unto, implying movement toward a certain point, and *zēlóō* (2206), to be desirous,
zealous. From this we have the English word "zeal." The compound verb means to make jealous or provoke to jealousy. In the
Old Testament, idolatry was conceived as adultery, figuratively
speaking, because Jehovah was viewed as the husband of Israel.
He had chosen Israel for Himself, performing miracles and
signs as expressions of His love and devotion. Israel, however, did
not respond with the same love and commitment. God's love
proved to be one-sided, and thus Israel was considered as an un-
faithful partner or prostitute. God is presented as a devoted husband against whom adultery has been perpetrated (Jer. 3:1–9;
Hos. 4). He wanted Israel to respond to His love and to be
totally committed to Him. It was the desire of God, when He
sent His Son into the world, that the people upon whom He had
showered so many blessings would be the first to wholeheartedly
accept Him, as if He were their husband and they were His
bride. Paul refers to this in 2 Corinthians 11:2: "For I am jealous over you with godly jealousy: for I have espoused you to one
husband, that I may present you as a chaste virgin to Christ."
Jealousy is associated with love. God's love, however, was rejected.
The rejection of Christ by the Jews (John 1:11) did not leave
God indifferent, but stirred Him to great grief. In His passion
to save man, God so loved the world that He sent His Son in the
Person of Jesus Christ to die on the cross for their sins (John
3:14–16). For this reason Paul asks the rhetorical question,
"Did not Israel know [*égnō*, the third person singular second
aorist active indicative of *ginōskō* {1097}, to know experien-
tially]?" (Rom. 10:19). This is equivalent to what John 1:11
declares: "He came unto His own, and His own received
[*parélabon*, the third person plural second aorist active indicative
of *paralambánō* {3880}, to welcome] Him not." It is in this
sense that we understand Exodus 20:5, "For I the Lord thy

God am a jealous God." God gave Himself fully and unreservedly to Israel in the Person of His Son, the Lord Jesus Christ, but He was rejected. To this rejection, He did not react indifferently, but with passion. Likewise, God's passion was aroused in the wilderness while Moses was on the mount receiving the Ten Commandments from God for Israel. In such a short period of time, the Israelites fell into idolatry (Ex. 20:4; Deut. 4:15–19), and God's jealousy was provoked.

When God's Zeal to Save Turns to Anger

The only other places that the compound verb *parazēlóō*, to provoke to anger or jealousy, occurs is in Romans 10:19; 11:11, 14. This indicates that the Jews brought God to the point where His fervent zeal to save them turned from Israel to the Gentiles. Romans 10:19 is taken from Deuteronomy 32:21 which was Moses' song just before the Israelites entered Canaan. Moses said, "They have moved me to jealousy with that which is not God; they have provoked me to anger with their vanities: and I will move them to jealousy with those which are not a people; I will provoke them to anger with a foolish nation." In Romans 10:19, Paul quotes Moses saying, "I will provoke you to jealousy [*parazēlōsō*, the first person singular future active indicative of *parazēlóō*] by them that are no people [*ep'* for the preposition *epi* {1909} meaning concentrating upon; *ouk* {3756}, the absolute 'not'; *éthnei*, the dative singular neuter form of *éthnos* {1484}, nation, meaning them who have not yet acquired the status of a nation or the Gentiles in general], and by a foolish nation I will anger [*parorgiō̆*, the first person singular future active indicative of *parorgízō* {3949} from *pará*, at the point of, unto, implying movement toward a certain point, and *orgízō* {3710}, to anger, irritate] you." And then in verse 20, Paul quotes Isaiah 65:1: "I was found of them that sought Me not; I was made manifest unto them that asked not after Me." In

Romans 11:14, for the third time Paul uses the verb *parazēlaȓ*, saying, "If by any means I may provoke to emulation them which are my flesh [the Jews], and might save some of them." This indicates that only individual Jews, and not the nation as a whole, shall accept the Lord Jesus as the Messiah during the times of the Gentiles (Rom. 11:25).

Idolatry Offends God

We must remember that in 1 Corinthians 10:22 Paul is comparing the behavior of the Gentile Christians with the Jews of old. As they provoked God to jealousy through their rejection of Him and caused Him to turn toward the Gentiles, He divorced them, so to speak, since they did not respond to His love and commitment to them. He will deal likewise with the so-called believers who continue to attend the idolatrous feasts of the heathen. Paul declares, in other words, that the individual who continues to practice idolatry is not a true Christian. It is to be noted that the verb *parazēloúmen* is in the present active indicative form, which means to **continue** to provoke God to jealousy by persisting in idolatrous practices. Paul includes himself in this by saying "we," and this is why he has it in the present active indicative. He, himself, could not be a real believer if he were to practice idolatry. Idolatry is communion with demons, and demons are a rebellious force opposed to God as revealed by Jesus Christ. God revealed by Jesus Christ, is offended to be placed on the same level with idols and to be treated as an equal to the so-called gods of idolatrous practices. God's emotions were aroused and He was angered by the rejection of the Jews and their devotion to idolatrous practices; but how much more angry will He be if we compromise Christian worship with idolatrous practices! Unfortunately, much of Christendom has turned the worship of Christ into idol worship with its statues and images of the virgin Mary and saints.

In Corinth, there was a tendency among believers to participate in the Lord's Supper and also in the feasts of the idol temples. Let us note carefully the words of Isaiah 42:8: "I am the Lord: that is My name: and My glory will I not give to another, neither My praise to graven images." And then, in verse 17, Isaiah says, "They shall be turned back, they shall be greatly ashamed, that trust in graven images, that say to the molten images, 'You are our gods.'" To provoke the Lord to jealousy is just one step prior to provoking the Lord to anger. We see the fulfillment of this today in that the nation of Israel is angry and in conflict with its Gentile neighbors. In Deuteronomy 32:22, we find that the anger of God is the outcome of the justice of God: "For a fire is kindled in my anger, and shall burn unto the lowest hell, and shall consume the earth with her increase, and set on fire the foundations of the mountains" (see v. 21 also). The anger of God was manifested when God permitted twenty-three thousand to die (1 Cor. 10:8), when the disobedient Israelites were stung by the serpents (v. 9), and when they were destroyed by the destroyer (v. 10). Are not these examples of what takes place when we provoke the Lord to jealousy and anger? We can expect the same treatment as a result of the justice of God when we pretend to follow Him and at the same time have fellowship with demons. We must beware in thinking we are strong Christians who can stand in the presence of evil, when in reality our strength is pure stubbornness, and we fall.

The answer, then, to the first question of 1 Corinthians 10:22 is yes, we are provoking the Lord to jealousy and we can expect His wrath to be manifested upon us if we do not flee from evil.

"Are We *Inherently* Stronger Than He Is?"

What does the Apostle mean by his second question, "Are we stronger than He?" The answer necessitated by the relative *mē*

(3361) is no. Which part of the Trinity is spoken about here? In verse 9 it was Christ. The discussion in verse 21 deals with a Christian participating in the Lord's table and the feasts of idolatry. The Lord's table is Christ's table, for it was He who died for us, and Holy Communion is celebrated because of what He did for us. Therefore, the "He" here must be taken to mean Christ. God manifested His wrath toward the idolatrous practices of the Israelites, and He considers participation at the Lord's table and eating meats sacrificed to idols in the idol temple likewise a provocation to the Lord. Probably those who participated in idol feasts, like the Israelites of old, did not believe that God would show His anger toward them. Nevertheless, we find instances of those who participated lightly at the Lord's table and were struck dead (1 Cor. 11:30). This is why Paul says, "If we judged ourselves [*diekrínomen*, the first person plural imperfect active indicative of *diakrínō* {1252}, to exercise discernment], we should not be judged [*ekrinómetha*, the first person plural imperfect passive indicative of *krínō* {2919}, to judge, condemn]" (1 Cor. 11:31). Such proud and obstinate people, thinking that they are strong Christians who can safely participate in idol feasts, are not strong at all. Sooner or later, they will fall. I well remember a young lady who had fallen into sin with a young man she knew. She cried bitter tears over her sin, and my wife and I advised her to stay as far away from him as possible. What did she do? She got a job just a block away from where he was working so she could prove to herself that she could resist temptation. You know what happened. The Bible tells us to flee from fornication and the devil—not to place ourselves directly in its path. The Lord knows our human frailties, and He does not want us to put ourselves in a position where we are tempted above our ability to stand.

The word for "stronger" is *ischuróteroi*, the nominative plural masculine comparative adjective of *ischurós* (2478), inherently strong. The noun form of this word is *ischús* (2479), strength which is inherent power. This is contrasted to the word *dúnamis* (1411), executive power or power to accomplish. The difference in the meaning of the words is indicated in Philippians 4:13: "I can do [*ischúō* {2840}, meaning I have the inherent power or I have been given divine power by Christ] all things through Christ who strengthens [*endunamoúnti*, the dative singular masculine present active participle of *endunamóō* {1743}, to make able to accomplish anything, derived from *en* {1722}, in, and *dunamóō* {1412}), to strengthen, related to the noun *dúnamis*] me." The proud Christians who participated in the idol feasts thought that they were inherently strong or divinely enabled, but this was certainly not an accomplishment of the Christian grace of *diákrisis* (1253), discernment (1 Cor. 12:10). The answer, therefore, to the second question of 1 Corinthians 10:22 is a definite no. Such stubborn Christians think that they are stronger than Christ (*ischuróteroi*, the comparative degree of *ischurós* inherently strong), but they are not. "Let him that thinks he stands beware lest he fall" (1 Cor. 10:12).

LESSONS:

1. God is a jealous God in that He became offended when His absolute love and commitment to Israel were refused (John 1:11).
2. As there was a figurative marriage union between Israel and God, so is there a union between the believer and Christ. If we, as believers, reject Christ's love and salvation, we provoke Him not only to jealousy, but to wrath.
3. The wrath of the Lord Jesus Christ may not be manifested immediately, but it is stored up for the day of wrath (2 Cor. 5:10).
4. Our profession of belief in God must have a corresponding behavior, otherwise such a profession is presumption. A Christian who does not conform to a holy life, although perhaps not punished immediately, ultimately will have to account to God.

1 Cor. 10:23 | *Our Lives Should Give to the Common Good*

> *All things are permissible to me, but all things do not contribute to the common good. All things are permissible to me, but not all things build up.*

The subject of 1 Corinthians, chapters 8, 9, and 10, is whether or not Christians should participate in the eating of meats which had been sacrificed to idols. These meals were commonly available in an idolatrous city like Corinth (1 Cor. 8:1). They were probably of a better quality and a lower price than other meats, and so it was a temptation for the believers to buy them.

Paul, finding himself faced with this problem, presents his thesis that eating or not eating meats sacrificed to idols is a matter of the individual conscience of each believer. In 1 Corinthians 8:1–13, he tells us to be sensitive to our own conscience, but to understand that conscience is an intuitive knowledge given by the Holy Spirit indwelling us. It tells us whether something is right or wrong.

In 1 Corinthians 9:1–18, Paul gives us the example of his own life as being one of privation and self-denial.

In 1 Corinthians 9:19–23, he tells us that the motivating power of such denial was his consummate desire to lead souls to Christ, and in 1 Corinthians 9:24–27, he tells us that such a life of denial will surely have a crown and a reward at the end of the race.

Then in 1 Corinthians 10:1–13 Paul illustrates the race of the Christian with the wilderness journey of the Israelites. He warns us that God must not be tested and that He has a way of imposing retribution upon those who fail. We must not, however, mistake the example that Paul gives of the Israelites as a model of the believer, but rather as a sample of the patience and longsuffering of God towards both believers and unbelievers. What he presents in these verses is a historical commentary on the attitude of God expressed in Romans 2:4–6: "Or do you despise the riches of His goodness and forbearance and longsuffering; not knowing that the goodness of God leads you to repentance? But after your hardness and impenitent heart, you treasure up unto yourself wrath against the day of wrath and revelation of the righteous judgment of God; who will render to every man according to his deeds."

In 1 Corinthians 10:14–22 Paul castigates the practice of so-called Christians who partake of the Lord's Supper and, at the same time, participate in the heathen banquets where animals had been sacrificed to idols. He ends this paragraph with a question for those who practice such compromise: "Are we stronger than He?" referring to Christ, of course. This was asked in order to overthrow the claim made by participants in idol worship that they were strong and, no matter what they did, they would not fall into sin or lose their faith. In such a case, intransigence is mistaken for faith. The argument of the Apostle Paul is that if they engaged in such practices of idolatry, they were not really true Christians. We never find Christ, who lived the majority of His early life in Galilee which neighbored the Gentile world, in any way compromising with idolatry.

In 1 Corinthians 10:23–11:1, Paul gives us rules that can serve as guidelines for individual decisions as to what is permissible and what is not in our redeemed lives.

It is necessary to consider these arguments as we examine the last paragraph of Paul's long discussion pertaining to what is permissible in the Christian life and what is not. Understanding these regulations will help us as children of God to make correct decisions.

"All Things Are Permissible to Me, but All Things Do Not Contribute to the Common Good"

Verse 23 bears a great similarity to 1 Corinthians 6:12, but is more general. The Textus Receptus and the Majority Text have both verses exactly the same. However, while the critical texts (UBS and the Nestle's Text) have *moi*, "to me," the dative singular first person form of the personal pronoun *egō* (1473), I, in 1 Corinthians 6:12, it is missing in 1 Corinthians 10:23. We prefer to include "to me" since Paul is speaking here about the individual Christian's authority and prerogative to make personal judgments about specific things that do not pertain to his eternal salvation. The believer belongs to the Body of Christ, and he ought to consider how every decision affects not only his own life, but also all the other members of that Body. While 1 Corinthians 6:12 says that all things are permissible to an individual as a child of God, he should be careful not to allow anything to have controlling authority over him.

"All Things Are Permissible to Me, but Not All Things Build Up"

Here in 1 Corinthians 10:23, Paul adds a more noble reason why the believer should not do some things which might be otherwise permissible. He says, "But not all things build up [*oikodomeí*, the third person singular present active indicative of *oikodoméō*

{3618}, to build up]." The verb *oikodoméō* and the noun *oikodomḗ* (3619) are used to refer to the Christian Church and its members and are compared to a building, a temple of God, erected upon the one and only foundation, Jesus Christ (1 Cor. 3:9–11). To show that this "building up" has Jesus Christ as its foundation, we find in 1 Corinthians 3:10 (twice), 12, 14 the compound verb *epoikodoméō* (2026) which comes from *epí* (1909), upon, and *oikodoméō*, to build. The noun *oikodomḗ*, when it refers to a physical building, means a building that is in the process of construction (Matt. 24:1). Every Christian is in the process of being built until the very day of his death, and we who are brothers in Christ ought to contribute positively to each one's moral and spiritual edification. Whatever we say and do in our lives has an effect upon fellow believers. While we may not have had any part in the foundation, we can certainly affect the superstructure either negatively or positively. The Apostle Paul is claiming here that everything we choose to do in our lives should have a positive, constructive effect on the lives of other Christians. After all, we belong to the same body of Christ (1 Cor. 12:13). When Christians see a fellow believer partaking of meat that had been offered to idols, will these Christians be built up in their faith, whether they are strong or feeble, or will they be offended and fail in their discernment or determination? Paul makes it clear that Christians should avoid activities which could cause a brother in Christ to stumble.

But what about other practices which do not have a regulatory prohibition? In our modern society, we should consider drinking, dancing, watching suggestive movies or TV programs, immodest dress, and so on, as harming the Body of Christ. Some of these practices could be considered flirtation with idolatry in that they are Satan-inspired and demon-controlled (10:20). If these activities have anything to do with demons and satanic practices, without doubt they ought to be completely avoided. If they do not, however, we should ask the question, Will such practices cause my fellow believers to be edified and grow in the Lord? If not, my own personal decision should be to avoid these activities.

LESSONS:

1. The Christian should never be guided by the philosophy that others do it, why can't I?
2. The guiding questions should be, Will my doing a certain thing lead others to believe I am stubborn or will they mistake my stubbornness for faith? Will what I do affect others adversely?
3. Our whole demeanor and dress should bring honor to the name of our Lord.

1 Cor. 10:24 | *No Christian Should Seek His Own Advantage*

Let no one continue to seek his own selfish good, but each one the good of another who is different.

In the previous verse, Paul has told us that while many things may be permissible for the Christian, it is not wise for him to live a life of reckless abandonment to self-satisfaction. To be pleasing to his heavenly Father, a Christian must pick and choose that which builds up not only himself, but also others who are members of the body of Christ.

"Let No One Continue to Seek"

The Apostle Paul now lays down a general principle: "Let no one continue to seek his own selfish good." "Let no one" is *mēdeís* (3367) which is derived from *mḗ* (3361), the relative "not," and *heís* (1520), one. Paul makes this a relative negative because he knows that believers, although indwelt by the nature of God (2 Pet. 1:4), are still human, even as he was, confessing that sin dwelt in him even after his salvation (Rom. 7:20). The absolute "no one" could have been expressed by the use of *oudeís* (3762). However that would not be realistic, for although we are not of the world, we continue to be in the world (John 17:14). This principle constitutes an individual responsibility of the believer, which is why it is expressed in the singular form.

145

The verb "seek" is *zēteítō*, the third person singular present active imperative of *zētéō* (2212), seek. The active present tense indicates continuity, so we have translated this imperative, "Let no one **continue** to seek his own selfish good." If the advice were to avoid seeking something particular for oneself, it would not have been the present imperative *zēteítō*, but the aorist imperative *zētēsátō*, as in 1 Peter 3:11. Paul is admonishing believers here that the life of the Christian should not be one of constantly seeking his own selfish benefit, as Lot did when his uncle, Abraham, said to him,

> Let there be no strife, I pray you, between me and you, and between my herdmen and your herdmen; for we are brethren. Is not the whole land before you? Separate yourself, I pray you, from me: if you will take the left hand, then I will go to the right; or if you depart to the right hand, then I will go to the left. And Lot lifted up his eyes, and beheld all the plain of Jordan, that it was well watered everywhere, before the Lord destroyed Sodom and Gomorrah, even as the garden of the Lord, like the land of Egypt, as you come unto Zoar. Then Lot chose him all the plain of Jordan; and Lot journeyed east: and they separated themselves the one from the other. Abraham dwelt in the land of Canaan, and Lot dwelt in the cities of the plain, and pitched his tent toward Sodom (Gen. 13:8–12).

Lot prospered and became the leader of Sodom (Gen. 19:1). In 2 Peter 2:7, 8, Lot is called "just" or "righteous" (*dikaios* [1342]). In Genesis 13:13, we read, "But the men of Sodom were wicked and sinners before the Lord exceedingly." Lot succeeded in becoming their leader, but how his righteous soul (2 Pet. 2:8) must have pained him as he observed the iniquity of Sodom for which he could do nothing but lament. Ezekiel 16:49 tells us, "Behold, this was the iniquity of your sister Sodom, pride, fullness of bread, and abundance of idleness was in her and in her daughters, neither did she strengthen the hand of the poor and needy." Success frequently involves voluntary compromise and involuntary reaping of the consequences of compromise.

"His Own Selfish *Good*"

There is no noun after the definite reflexive pronoun *tó heautoú* (1438), of himself. Thus we have, "Let him not continue to seek his own selfish," and the noun could be "good," "interest," "end," or whatever characterized the Christian's selfishness. In the case of Lot and Abraham, Lot sought his own ease and comfort in the rich and fertile land (Gen. 13:10). A Christian should not seek a life of ease and comfort, but a selfless life that will benefit others. Selfishness, whenever chosen, must bear its consequences as it did with Lot. Not only did he rule over wicked people, but he lost his own family, for he ended up committing abominable sin with his daughters resulting in the birth of Moab and Ammon. These two became the heads of two evil groups of people, the Moabites and the Ammonites. Thus, the selfish decision of Lot had consequences which were lasting and could not be effaced. Paul urges us not make a selfish decision at any time. We must never give self the preeminent position in our lives, but we should rather give it to God who indwells us. Let us never lose sight that our example is being followed by the other members of the body of Christ with whom we are joined together.

"But Each One"

"But" is expressed by the adversative particle *allá* (235) which is more emphatic than the particle *dé* (1161), but. This is the antithetical particle used in 1 Corinthians 6:11 to show the transformation which God alone brings about in the human being by redeeming him from the worst possible sinful life. First Corinthians 6:9–11a says,

> Know you not that the unrighteous shall not inherit the kingdom of God? And such were some of you. Be not deceived: neither fornicators, nor idolaters, nor adulterers, nor effeminate, nor abusers of

themselves with mankind, nor thieves, nor covetous, nor drunkards, nor revilers, nor extortioners, shall inherit the kingdom of God. And such were some of you:

Then he goes on to say, "But you are washed, but you are sanctified, but you are justified in the name of the Lord Jesus, and by the Spirit of our God." This word "but" is *allá*, an emphatic particle. The only way that a human being can change from self-centeredness to God-centeredness, whereby God becomes first and paramount in his life, is through the transforming power of the Holy Spirit.

In the second phrase of our verse, the Textus Receptus and the Majority Text have the subject as *hékastos* (1538), each one separately as an individual. The critical texts, including the United Bible Society and the Nestle's Text, do not have this adjective. The work of grace is done in individual hearts and never in groups per se. Whenever the inclusiveness of individuals is to be stressed, the adjective *pás* (3956), whosoever, is used as in John 3:16, "For God so loved the world that He gave His only begotten Son, that whosoever [*pás*, whosoever as an individual, but none is to be excluded] believes on Him should not perish but have everlasting life."

The verb *zēteítō*, to seek continuously, which is used in the first part of the verse, should be implied in the second part. It concerns the varying attitude of selflessness in the lives of believers, and selflessness is a work of grace accomplished by the death of Christ on the cross. Romans 6:6 declares, "Knowing this, that our old man is crucified with Him, that the body of sin might be destroyed, that henceforth we should not serve sin." Our "old man" includes self, and God is the only One who can accomplish the crucifixion of self. The difference between a believer and an unbeliever is that the believer has had self crucified with Christ and by Christ. This, however, is representative of the basic work of grace. It is the fruit of the Spirit of God (Gal. 5:22, 23). Each individual fruit, however, varies from the others. Some are juicy and sweet while others are not. If one examines oranges on a tree, he will find that they are not all the same in their size and taste. The tastiness of fruit depends on many things, such as the care given by the fruitgrower and the soil in which it is grown.

Paul, in Galatians 2:20, says, "I have crucified myself with Christ [*sunestaúrōmai*, the first person singular perfect middle indicative of *sustauróō* {4957}]." This is the only instance in the New Testament that this form of the verb is used. We must examine, then, whether it means a voluntary crucifixion with Jesus Christ which we continue to accomplish consequent to the effective work of Christ who crucified us with Himself on the cross. In Galatians 5:24, Paul says, "And they that are Christ's have crucified [*estaúrōsan*, the third person plural aorist active indicative of *stauróō* {4717}, crucify] the flesh with the affections and lusts." In Galatians 6:14, Paul says, "But God forbid that I should glory, save in the cross of our Lord Jesus Christ, by whom the world is crucified [*estaúrōtai*, the third person singular perfect middle indicative of *stauróō*, crucify] unto me, and I unto the world." Here it is evident that the work of Christ is fundamental and essential in our lives. That is, our crucifixion with Him on the cross must be followed by our conformity to the crucified life. Anyone who has not been crucified together with Christ on the cross cannot in any way crucify himself to the world, for the second is possible only in view of the first. One can see, therefore, that the adjective *hékastos*, each one, is essential to the whole teaching of this verse and of the New Testament. Our choice, therefore, of the inclusion of "each one" in this verse is valid and fully justified.

"*The Good* of Another *Who Is Different*"

The object of this phrase is implied. We have chosen to presume it to be the "good" or that which one would desire for himself. The advice of Paul is that we, as believers, should desire for others that which we desire for ourselves. However, it is a temptation to desire for others the good that we desire for ourselves only if they are in agreement with our principles and our objectives. But the word for "another" here is *hetérou*, the genitive singular masculine form of the adjective *héteros* (2087), another of a different kind, as in verse 29. This stands in contrast to *állos* (243), meaning another arithmetically, but of the same kind. The desire of God, Jesus Christ, and the apostles is that our lives may be structured to be possessing the character of God in constantly seeking that which is good, not only for ourselves, but for others who may differ from us. The Lord reminded us in Matthew 5:43–48:

> You have heard that it has been said, 'Thou shalt love thy neighbor, and hate thine enemy.' But I say unto you, love your enemies, bless them that curse you, do good to them that hate you, and pray for them which despitefully use you, and persecute you; that you may be the children of your Father which is in heaven: for He makes His sun to rise on the evil and on the good, and sends rain on the just and on the unjust. For if you love them which love you, what reward have you? Do not even the publicans the same? And if you salute your brethren only, what do you more than others? Do not even the publicans the same? Be you therefore perfect, even as your Father which is in heaven is perfect.

One way to be like our Father is to wish that which is good for others. And others include the ones who are different from us, our enemies, and those who are unjust. This is the work of Jesus Christ and His cross, but it must also become our conscious endeavor. And it can become a conscious effort only because of what Christ has done for us and in us.

LESSONS:

1. The reason that the Apostle Paul does not use the absolute *oudeís*, no one, instead of the relative *mēdeís*, no one, is because only God is perfectly selfless.

2. Paul is endeavoring to instill in the hearts of the Corinthians the character of selflessness and not merely an occasional act of selflessness by using the verb *zeteítō* in the present imperative form, which indicates a continual action.

3. When we become believers, we must not expect everybody to be like us with the same attitudes and character. People are different (*héteroi*).

4. However, we must learn to wish for those who are different the same good that we would wish for ourselves.

5. In view of Romans 8:28, we must understand "good" (*agathón* [18], good, benevolent) as being everything that God brings into our lives as occurring for the ultimate purpose of our conformity or the conformity of others to Himself.

1 Cor. 10:25

Living in a World You Cannot Control

Everything that is on sale in a butcher shop, keep eating, making no investigation for conscience sake,

Corinth was a cosmopolitan heathen city. In the butcher shops they sold meat which had been slaughtered for sale to the public, and also that which was left over from the animals sacrificed in heathen temples. Christian believers faced a dilemma. What were they to do when they were shopping for meat?

"Everything That Is on Sale in a Butcher Shop, Keep Eating"

Paul provides a guideline. When you go to the marketplace where meats and other foodstuffs are exhibited for sale, do not inquire or investigate to learn which meats were sacrificed to idols in order to appease your conscience. Feel free to buy and eat whatever is sold.

"Making No Investigation for Conscience Sake"

A modern day example of this problem is the selection of a bank for your financial affairs. What banks should Christians deal with? The answer is banks that are honest and are not known for dishonest practices. However, a bank may also have the accounts of businesses with which our Christian conscience does not agree. Unless it is a commonly known fact that a bank specializes in such businesses, it is not necessary to begin an investigative process as to whether all the customers of a bank would be approved by our conscience before we bank with them. We must recognize that we live in a wicked and complex world. No matter how careful we may be, we cannot completely separate ourselves from the world, but we should not voluntarily contaminate ourselves with it.

There are innumerable other examples. Consider, for instance, the matter of paying taxes. Every Christian will agree that there are things our taxes pay for with which we vehemently disagree. Abortion is one such example. What shall we do? Inquire as to how the last penny of our taxes will be spent before we file our tax return? We would be fully justified in our objection. In Matthew 17:24–27, we find how the Lord dealt with this problem of paying taxes: "And when they were come to Capernaum, they that received tribute money [taxes] came to Peter, and said, 'Does not your Master pay tribute [taxes]?'" Note what the Lord said to Peter: "'Of whom do the kings of the earth take custom or tribute? Of their own children, or of strangers?' Peter said unto him, 'Of strangers.' Jesus said unto him, 'Then are the children free.'" Jesus was the Son of God and therefore exempt. But observe what He added: "Notwithstanding, lest we should offend [*skandalísōmen*, the first person plural aorist active subjunctive of *skandalízō* {4624}, to offend, scandalize] them, you go to the sea, and cast a hook, and take up the fish that first comes up; and when you have opened his mouth, you shall find a piece of money: that take and give unto them for Me and you."

In spite of the fact that Jesus believed that He along with Peter should not pay taxes, He made provision to pay them through a miracle so that He might not become offensive to the world which He came to redeem. How wonderful it would be if we could handle our taxes that way, or if they amounted to only one coin, but the world has become much more complex since the time of Christ, and we are entrapped in it and must do whatever would best please our heavenly Master.

When the Christian came to the marketplace in Corinth, he was found in a similar situation. What was Paul's advice? He should not make extensive inquiries in order to absolve his conscience. The more one probes, the more he will find himself to be in disagreement with what is going on in the world, and the more confused and frustrated he will become. The Christian is in the world, but he is not part of it.

LESSONS:

1. As a Christian, understand that you cannot research and investigate everything, otherwise you will become totally confused and frustrated.
2. It is unrealistic to take the initiative to investigate everything in the world in which you must participate.
3. It was not necessary for a Christian living in Corinth to make himself obnoxious by probing questions every time he went to the marketplace or the butcher shop to buy meat.
4. If we know, however, that something is inconsistent with our principles, we will do well to avoid that problem area.

| 1 Cor. 10:26 | *Christians May Enjoy God's Blessings* |

For the earth is the Lord's and the fullness thereof.

The idolaters who lived in Corinth sacrificed animals to idols. Some would-be Christians considered that feasting on sacrificed animals in the idol temples with the idolaters was not in violation of Christian principles. Paul adamantly opposed this practice. He told them to flee from idolatry and have nothing to do with it. But he maintained that this conduct was entirely different than going to the marketplace and buying meat without asking questions.

While there were those who had an indifferent attitude regarding meats sacrificed to idols, evidently there were others whose consciences were so tender they were caught in an impass. Paul assures them that in reality, everything belongs to God and comes from His gracious hand. "For every creature of God is good, and nothing to be refused, if it be received with thanksgiving" (1 Tim. 4:4).

"For the Earth Is the Lord's and the Fullness Thereof"

This quotation is taken from Psalm 24:1. Apparently, it was a well-known quotation of the Old Testament, and it was not necessary for Paul to mention that it constituted one of David's psalms.

LESSONS:

1. Whatever God has provided that is healthy and good belongs to the Christian to enjoy.
2. Because there are idolaters who sacrifice animals does not mean that what remains of those animals and is sold in the open market cannot be bought and enjoyed by the people of the Lord.

1 Cor. 10:27

Eating with Unbelievers

If one of the unbelievers invites you, and you want to go, everything that is set before you, eat, making no investigation for conscience sake.

In verses 25 and 26 Paul explains that since everything that is in the world is the Lord's and the fullness thereof, the Corinthian Christian could feel free to go to the marketplace and buy meat without asking questions and investigating its source in order that his conscience might not trouble him.

"If One of the Unbelievers Invites You"

Paul now discusses another possibility that faced the Christians. Suppose you receive a dinner invitation from one of your unbelieving acquaintances. Some have suggested that this may refer to private restaurants which tried to attract both Christians and non-Christians. It would be anybody's guess where the meat they served came from. This possibility is quite plausible in a place like Corinth which was a cosmopolitan city. In Acts 18:2 we find that many Jews came from Rome. However, it may have been a nonbelieving relative or a heathen person whom the believer was trying to influence for Christ. We cannot be certain, for the verse starts with the suppositional conjunction *ei* (1487), if, indicating a mere subjective possibility separate from all experience. Paul makes the supposition in order to draw a conclusion as to what one's attitude should be.

Who does "one of the unbelievers" refer to? The first thing that we must understand is that this is not any particular person. In reality, it makes no difference who that person is. But there is one thing that is certain—he is one of the unbelievers (*tís* [5100], anyone, a masculine enclitic indefinite pronoun; *apístōn*, the genitive plural masculine form of the adjective *ápistos* [571], unbeliever, one without faith [*pístis* {4102}, here meaning the faith of Jesus Christ]). This could be either an unbelieving Jew or an unbelieving heathen. The word *ápistos*, unbeliever, occurs eleven times in 1 Corinthians and three times in 2 Corinthians, while in the rest of the New Testament it occurs only nine times.

The "you" in the phrase "invites you" refers to a believer in Jesus Christ, no matter of what background, Jewish or heathen. The verb for "invite" is *kaleí*, the third person singular present active indicative of *kaléō* (2564), to call, to invite, particularly to a banquet or meal (Matt. 22:3, 9; John 2:2). The supposition then is that someone from among the unbelieving acquaintances invites a believer to eat in his home or guest house.

"And You Want to Go"

"And you want" is translated from *kai* (2532), and; *thélete*, the second person plural present active indicative of *thélō* (2309), to want, wish. This matter pertains to the inclination of the Christian. He is free to refuse or to accept. It is a decision which he must make for himself.

In the earthly life of Jesus Christ, the unbelieving Pharisees opposed the Lord and His ministry. We find, however, that on three occasions they invited Him to come to their homes to eat with them and He accepted. The first instance is found in Luke 7:36. This passage relates an occasion when a sinful woman found Him in that particular house and broke an alabaster vase of precious ointment with which she annointed the feet of the Lord Jesus Christ. Thus, the acceptance of an invitation to eat with the Pharisees became an opportunity for the acceptance of the worship of a sinful woman and a beautiful testimony to the Pharisees.

The second invitation which the Lord received to eat at the house of a Pharisee is found in Luke 11:37–39. He accepted that invitation disregarding the possibility of being branded as a compromiser. He used the occasion, however, to teach the people present that washing one's hands (the word is *ebaptísthe*, the third person singular aorist indicative passive of *baptízō* [907], to baptize, to dip) is not equivalent to having the heart cleansed.

In the third instance in which the Lord was invited to eat with a Pharisee, he healed a man suffering from dropsy (Luke 14:1–4).

The conclusion, then, that we may draw is that it is not wrong to go to an unbeliever's house for a meal, but we must be Christlike and take advantage of every opportunity to show our benevolence but not compromise with the customs and practices of unbelief. In each case relating to our Lord, a lesson had been taught.

Thus it seems that the acceptance of an invitation to eat at an unbeliever's house is a matter left entirely to the judgment of the individual believer and must be counted as one of the indifferent matters (*adiáphora*), as was going to the common market to buy meat (1 Cor. 10:25).

The verb "to go" is *poreúesthai*, the present middle deponent infinitive of *poreúomai* (4198), to go. Both the verb *thélete* and *poreústhai* are in the present tense which indicate that this is not a rare invitation, but a repeated one. Paul is making this supposition of a repeated invitation being accepted to draw a conclusion from it.

"Everything That Is Set Before You, Eat"

The first conclusion is to eat everything that is set before you. "Everything" is *pán*, the accusative singular neuter form of the adjective *pás* (3956), meaning all the foods that the host has put on the table to be consumed by his guests. The scene this time has changed from the marketplace where a particular piece of meat is bought to the table in the house of the host.

". . . that is set before you" is *tó*, the accusative singular neuter of the article *ho* (3588), the; *paratithémenon*, the accusative singular neuter present passive participle of *paratíthēmi* (3908), to put or place near someone. It is a common practice of a host to place many varieties of food on the table for consumption by the guests. Should a Christian at that time ask questions regarding the food such as where it was bought and whether or not it was sacrificed to idols? This is not the time to ask such questions. If the guests had any doubt about the propriety of eating the food that the host would give them, they should not have accepted the invitation at all. The same is true insofar as selecting the marketplace and the butcher from which one buys his meat. Paul's conclusion is that a person should not be rude in questioning the host about matters that he should have settled in his mind before going to the home. Once the Christian has accepted the invitation, even if it is an invitation extended by an unbeliever, he should not behave in an unbecoming manner.

"Eat" is *esthíete*, the second person plural present active imperative of *esthíō* (2068), to eat. Sitting in the house at the dinner table is not the time to ask questions and investigate the source of the meat. What an offense that would be to the unbelieving host! The Apostle Paul is not against the protection of the Christian conscience as to what food one should eat, but there are certain times when questions can offend and do not demonstrate sincere love. In 1 Corinthians 13:5, Paul says of Christian love that it "does not behave itself unseemly [*ouk* {3756}, the absolute 'not'; *aschēmoneí*, to misbehave, the third person singular present active indicative of *aschēmoneō* {807} derived from the privative *a* {1}; and *schēma* {4976}, outward shape, figure]." After all, a love for souls and a desire to win them to Christ should be the motivating power (1 Cor. 9:22). Paul wanted to do everything that he could without compromising character and principle to win the idolaters to Christ. Every time he accepted an invitation to a heathen's house and table, it would be with the purpose of winning souls to Christ. His desire is the same for all of us and all the Corinthian Christians. What he was telling the Corinthians in 10:25, 27 is that questions asked at the wrong time can be odious and offensive to those to whom they are submitted. If a Christian's conscience is tender about what is permissible and what is not, he ought to determine his position beforehand and act accordingly. Above everything else, he ought to practice Christian love, the characteristic of which is that it does not behave in an unseemly manner.

The truth should never be compromised, but as to how and when it is proclaimed is a matter of proper discernment. If a person asks questions merely to show his religiosity he is demonstrating pride, and such pride can be disastrous to the cause of Christ. Another verb that is characteristic of the divine love that exists in the heart of the believer, and which is presented in 1 Corinthians 13:4, is "vaunteth not itself" (*perpereúetai*). This verb is not used elsewhere in the New Testament. *Perpereúomai* (4068) is a verb that carries the idea of arrogance along with proud behavior. It is putting self first and foremost. Such would be a believer who goes about in the marketplace and asks every butcher whether he sells meats sacrificed to idols or not, and who accepts a dinner invitation and waits until he sits at the table to

ask the host whether or not there is anything served that orig-
inates from animals sacrificed to idols.

"Making No Investigation for Conscience Sake"

The verb used here is *anakrínontes*, the nominative plural masculine present active participle of *anakrínō* (350). This indicates that the investigation is carried out at the time just before
eating, which, of course, is the improper time. The only motive
for asking is to be certain that there is nothing that would vio-
late the conscience of the believer. This precludes questioning on
other grounds such as whether any foods are served which were
prepared with ingredients to which one, for instance, may be allergic. Truth sometimes uses brutal methods and words to de-
fend itself, and when it becomes void of love, it becomes, as the
Apostle Paul says, "As sounding brass, or a tinkling cymbal"
(1 Cor. 13:1).

LESSONS:

1. It is not wrong to accept invitations to eat with unbelievers.
2. It is a matter of personal responsibility as to how we respond to those invitations.
3. In proclaiming the truth, we should show neither pride nor arrogance.
4. We should consider ahead of time the culture of the places we go, so as
   not to be in offense after we discover the nature of the places.

1 Cor. 10:28

If We Know, What Should We Do?

> *But if someone were to say to you, "This is meat sacrificed to idols," do not continue to eat because of him who informed you and the conscience. "For the earth is the Lord's and the fullness thereof."*

In the previous verse, Paul advised the Corinthian Christians not to behave in an obnoxious manner when visiting in the home of an unbeliever. He now gives specific advice for specific situations.

"But if Someone Were to Say to You, 'This Is Meat Sacrificed to Idols'"

The "if" (*ei* [1487]) of verse 27 is subjective, making the entire event hypothetical. Although the situation in that verse is a hypothesis, in this verse the realistic *eán* (1437), if, is used with *eípē*, the third person singular second aorist active subjunctive form of *légō* (3004), to say. Again, Paul presupposes a situation so that he may suggest the proper conclusion in such a matter.

But to whom does the "someone" (*tis* [5100], the nominative singular masculine indefinite pronoun) refer? It cannot be the person of verse 27 who was invited by an unbeliever to dinner. This is another one, rather, who is also a guest and knows where the host bought the meat and reveals its source. Whether or not the information is true is not revealed. He simply says, "This meat has been sacrificed to idols." The Textus Receptus and Majority Text use the word *eidōlóthuton* (1494), used in 1 Corinthians 8:1, 4, 7, 10. The United Bible Society and Nestle's Text use another word occurring nowhere else in the New Testament. It is *hieróthuton*, derived from the adjective *hierós* (2413), sacred, and *thúō* (2380), to sacrifice. The meaning of *eidōlóthuton* is an animal sacrificed to idols, while *hieróthuton* refers to something sacrificed to what people consider sacred.

What kind of person would thus inform the dinner party and more or less upgrade the *eidōlóthuton*, the animal sacrificed to idols, to *hieróthuton*, something sacred that had been sacrificed? Most probably it would not be a Christian who would be concerned lest another Christian might eat meat sacrificed to idols. It is unlikely that the terminology changed to *hieróthuton* from *eidōlóthuton*. Rather, it seems possible that this person is a Christian who enjoys gossiping about his fellow Christian's decision to accept an invitation to the house of an unbeliever and to eat what is set before him without asking any questions. Paul is not recommending here that we spread around what we know about our brethren. And certainly we should not if it is a matter nonessential to basic doctrine and moral life. In spite of gossiping about fellow Christians being wrong, the Apostle Paul gives his advice should such a case occur.

"Do Not Continue to Eat Because of Him Who Informed You and the Conscience"

Paul's advice is, "Do not continue to eat [*mḗ* {3361}, the relative 'not'; *esthíete*, the second person plural present active imperative of *esthíō* {2068}, to eat]." The supposition is that the Christians invited were eating already. Suddenly, an informer testifies that the meat they were eating had been sacrificed to idols. Paul says, "Do not continue to eat." And the reason for cessation is, "Because of him who informed *you.*" This is translated from *diá* (1223), because of; *ekeínon*, the accusative singular masculine demonstrative form of the pronoun *ekeínos* (1565), that one; *tón*, the accusative singular masculine of the article *ho* (3588), the; *mēnúsanta*, the accusative singular masculine aorist active participle of *mēnúō* (3377), to make known or disclose something previously unknown. Paul says to avoid eating for the sake of the Christian who gave the information, "and the conscience," meaning the conscience of the informer. Paul is concerned lest he be offended and stumble. In other words, Paul's advice is to stop eating rather than offend a brother, in spite of your disagreement with his distasteful behavior. Tattling should never be rewarded, but the principle here is that it is better to suffer deprivation of food than to offend a brother in Christ by eating what he considers offensive. While there may be complete disagreement with him, his objection should be respected. This law of love predominates the argument of Paul and is culminated in chapter 13.

"For the Earth Is the Lord's and the Fullness Thereof"

The Textus Receptus and Majority Text quote this verse from Psalm 24:1 which was first stated in verse 26. The critical texts do not repeat this quotation. Paul again stresses that everything comes from God and our acceptance or rejection of it should be made with a thankful heart and in the context of the influence our decision will have on others.

LESSONS:

1. In not every case should we insist on doing what we consider right.
2. That which is offensive to other Christians should be avoided.
3. Although we should accommodate those Christians who disagree with us, we should nevertheless uphold the principle of the freedom of the Christian life.

1 Cor. 10:29

Why Must One's Freedom Be Curtailed by Others?

But I am not speaking of his own conscience, but the one of another who is different. For why is my liberty judged by another's conscience?

God created everything good (Gen. 1:31), but man has corrupted the earth. Even such a necessity as meat which one may buy in the market could be polluted because it had been sacrificed to idols. This may present a problem to the Christian with a tender conscience, and Paul offers some guidelines on this subject.

"But I Am Not Speaking of His Own Conscience, but the One of Another *Who Is Different*"

The conscience to which Paul refers is not that of the Christian eating the meat (*tén*, the accusative singular feminine of the article *ho* [3588], the; *heautoú* [1438], himself), but that of another (*hetérou*, the genitive singular masculine form of the adjective *héteros* [2087], another). This word "another," however, implies another who is different than the one who eats. Thus we presume this informer probably has a different mentality than the first one invited to the dinner. It is one who believes that the Christian should not eat such meat as it may be a compromise with idol worship. The believer who argues that certain matters are nonessential (and this is one of them) should allow a certain latitude of choice in behavior.

"For Why Is My Liberty Judged by Another's Conscience?"

Paul, now assuming the role of the Christian invited to dinner, says, "For why is my liberty judged by another's conscience?" The word for "another" here is *állēs*, the genitive singular feminine form of the adjective *állos* (243), numerically another but of the same kind. It refers to the conscience of another fellow Christian.

Paul declares the independence of his own conscience, but maintains that more significant than his independence is his love for those who belong to the same community of Christians. Christians have a redeemed conscience, but there is room for each one to develop variably by the grace of God.

To be judged by another's conscience means to form or express an opinion as to where someone else stands insofar as his relationship to God is concerned. Such judgment is usually unfavorable. One Christian who chooses to act differently than another is often considered to be less intimately related to Christ. In this regard, we would do well to heed the words of our Lord: "Judge not according to the appearance, but judge righteous judgment" (John 7:24). Our judgment need not be dependent upon the judgment of others, but it must be correct, as our Lord said in Luke 12:57, "Yes, and why even of yourselves judge you not what is right?" Righteous judgment does not preclude independent judgment, but it has to be investigative and without prejudice.

LESSONS:

1. We should understand that unbelievers do have a conscience: "Having their conscience seared with a hot iron" (1 Tim. 4:2). It is wrong to say

that unbelievers do not have a conscience, but it is a conscience that is not regenerated by the Holy Spirit.

2. On the other hand, we recognize that believers have a different conscience, a basically benevolent (*agathē* [18]) and pure (1 Tim. 3:9; 2 Tim. 1:3) conscience (Acts 23:1; 1 Tim. 1:5, 19).

3. However, the Christian's conscience is pure and benevolent in various degrees. The Lord gives the nature of conscience, but man is responsible for the superstructure (1 Cor. 3:10).

4. The believer must maintain the independent judgment of his own conscience and not allow another's conscience to rule him.

5. Nevertheless, in the exercise of the independence of his own judgment, he ought to exercise the principle of love as elaborated in 1 Corinthians 13. He must be ready to forego his desires if that will strengthen his weaker brother (1 Cor. 8:7, 10, 12).

1 Cor. 10:30

Criticism for Gratitude

Since I by grace partake, why am I blasphemed for what I give thanks?

Even when one is living a dedicated life and is doing his utmost to win souls to Christ, he is often criticized. In fact, it often seems that the harder one tries to please and serve his Lord, the more evil is spoken of him. We see that even a servant as great as Paul suffered in the same manner.

"Since I by Grace Partake"

This verse begins with the suppositional conjunction *ei* (1487), which is the subjective "if," as does verse 27 also. However, we have translated the suppositional conjunction in this instance to mean "since." The context decides whether *ei*, if, suggests a supposition separate from all experience, indicating a mere subjective possibility. This is different from *eán* (1437), if, of realistic possibility and experience. But *ei* may also occupy the other extreme of the pendulum and provide a condition or contingency as to which there is no doubt and which can be translated as "since." In this case Paul presents himself as a guest in the house of an unbeliever. This acceptance by the Apostle Paul was bathed in the grace of God, for Paul was extremely careful not do anything but what that grace led him to do, in this particular case

173

counting it as a benevolent opportunity. We, therefore, prefer to maintain the basic meaning of "grace" (*cháris* [5485]). This is also part of the verb *eucharisteó* (2168), to be thankful, to give thanks. Without the grace of God there can be no true thanksgiving. The grace of God makes every gift of God acceptable with gratitude, recognizing that one does not deserve it, but has the privilege of receiving it.

When one is a recipient of the grace of God (*cháris*), he is also grateful. The dative *cháriti* is translated "by grace," implying the grace of God with which a saved person is filled, as was the Apostle Paul.

The phrase *cháriti metéchō* (3348), to have a share, to partake of, to participate in, is used only in verse 30. Paul implies that he, as a partaker of the grace of God, should also seize every opportunity to win a soul to Christ, such as an invitation by an unbeliever to join him in a meal. Grace compromises in nothing that is essentially sinful, but it will take advantage of every opportunity that may lead someone to Jesus Christ. This is the context in which Paul would consider an invitation to dinner at an unbeliever's house. Actually, the word *egó* (1473), I, a personal pronoun, is used emphatically here and should be translated "myself," or "I myself." Paul willingly accepted and used every opportunity that the grace of God presented to him.

"Why Am I Blasphemed?"

The criticism which Paul received from fellow believers must have grieved him. In verse 28 he states that his freedom to choose is not negotiable, although it is to be superceded by the law of love. This is why he asks the rhetorical question: "Why *then* am I evil spoken of?" This is translated from *blasphēmoúmai*, the first person singular present passive indicative of *blasphēméō* (987), to speak evil of, to defame, blaspheme. Why, Paul asks, is my reputation hurt by slander as if my decision to accept an invitation to eat at an unbeliever's house was not guided by grace.

"For What I Give Thanks"

This comes from the Greek *hupér* (5228), for, over; *hoú*, the genitive singular masculine relative form of the pronoun *hós* (3739), over which or for which; *egṓ*, I, myself, the first person singular pronoun which is used for the second time in this verse; and *eucharistṓ*, I give thanks or I am grateful. The intimation is that one moved by the grace of God should be grateful for that which it is permissible for him to have and should not be condemned.

LESSONS:

1. Paul is declaring here that this participation in a meal in the house of an unbeliever is part of the demonstration of the grace of God in his life. Nevertheless, he is criticized for doing it.
2. Therefore, Paul questions the criticism he received from fellow believers for doing something by the grace of God for which he is thankful.

The Basic Motivation of the Christian Life

And if you therefore eat and if you drink and if you do anything, do all things for the glory of God.

Paul now turns from specifics to generalities, and he makes clear why we should do what we do.

"And If You Therefore Eat and if You Drink and if You Do Anything"

The suppositional conjunction *eíte* (1535) from *ei* (1487), if, and *te* (5037), and, is used three times in this verse and should be translated "and if." The *oun* (3767), "therefore," provides the concluding remark by Paul based on the general discussion as to what a Christian should do when facing situations like the ones discussed in the previous chapter. Should a Christian take the initiative to inquire from the beginning of a social interchange whether or not meat sold in the market has been sacrificed to idols? When he is invited to dinner at the home of an unbeliever, should a Christian accept and eat everything that is placed before him or should he interrogate his host? What should he do if another Christian divulges that the meat served has been sacrificed to idols? In such a case, Paul's advice is that a Christian should quit eating it for the sake of the conscience of his fellow Christian. But what happens to his independent Christian conscience? Herein enters the principle of love. Do not insist on having your own way if it seeks to satisfy your selfish desire.

"Do All Things for the Glory of God"

Now Paul gives another guideline. If you eat or drink, which are things you will most likely do when you are invited to another home, or whatever you do, do it all for the glory of God.

This brings the matter of social contact out of the idol temple and into the environment of the home. The strict rule to flee from idolatry still stands (v. 14). If eating and drinking in the home environment draws you into idolatry and sin, then you are to flee from it. If, however, you can maintain social contact and be sure in your own conscience that you are not being drawn into sin, then you may go and do anything to the glory of God which is not sinful in itself.

But what is meant by "the glory of God?" "Glory" is the translation of *dóxa* (1391) from the verb *dokéō* (1380), to think, to rightly recognize. Whatever a Christian does in these suppositional situations should make others recognize that God indwells him. God is selfless, and selflessness should be seen in everyone who claims to be a child of God (v. 24).

Another important thing that a child of God should possess is respect for others, even if they are different from himself. Children of God should give the testimony that there is a oneness among them, although they may vary in minor viewpoints. However, such tolerance should not compromise with immorality or idolatry.

The purpose of a believer's actions is indicated here by the preposition *eis* (1519), into or unto, which is far more expressive than if it were indicated by the adverb *héneka* (1752), on account of or for the sake of. To bring glory to God is our purpose, and it should be sought aggressively in whatever we undertake to do in life. While "eating and drinking" refer to essential activities of life, they are not limited to that, since "all things" are indicated in *pánta*, the accusative plural neuter form of the adjective *pás* (3956), all, everything.

That this should be a constant guideline of life is indicated by the present tense of the three verbs, *esthíete*, eat; *pínete*, drink; and *poieíte*, do. This last verb occurs twice in our verse. It is the second person plural present active indicative of *poiéō* (4160), to do. This verb means to make, form, produce, bring about a cause, and is used to refer to any external act as manifested in the production of something tangible, corporeal, obvious to the senses, a completed action.

Colossians 3:17 says, "And whatsoever you do [*poiēte*, the present subjunctive] in word or deed, do all in the name of the Lord Jesus, giving thanks to God and the Father by Him." We can, therefore, glorify God by what we say and by what we do, and, in both cases, they should manifest what the name of the Lord Jesus stands for.

In Colossians 3:23 we are told how we should do all things for the glory of God: "And whatsoever you do, do it heartily [*ek* {1537}, out of, from; *psuchḗs*, the genitive of *psuchḗ* {5590}, soul] as to the Lord, and not unto men." If one believer decides to criticize another believer for having accepted an invitation to an unbeliever's house and brands him as a compromiser, what about our Lord? He accepted invitations to dinner in the Pharisee's homes (Luke 7:36; 11:37; 14:1) and also ate with publicans and sinners and the hated, dishonest tax collectors. For those who uphold legalism and criticize others for trivial matters, Paul's advice is that they should not mandate their way of life upon others. And as we pursue the freedom of our own conscience, we must remember what Paul wrote in 1 Corinthians 4:3: "But with me it is a very small thing that I should be judged of you [and we should keep it small and never blow it out of proportion], or of man's judgment: yes, I judge not my own self."

<u>LESSONS:</u>

1. In whatever you do, seek actively to promote the glory of God.
2. Live such an exemplary life that others will know that it is Christ who leads you to do what you do.
3. Recognize that there are things which are of themselves sinful, and they definitely should be avoided.

1 Cor. 10:32

Do Not Be a Stumbling Block

Continue to become inoffensive both to the Jews and to the Gentiles, and also to the church of God.

The illustration of the Christian running a race in 1 Corinthians 9:24–27 applies to the whole tenth chapter of 1 Corinthians. In his race, the Christian does not want others to hinder him. The believer is supposed to strive or struggle (*agōnízomai* [75], to agonize or strive for victory and to exercise self-control; *egkrateúetai*, the present tense of *egkrateúomai* [1467], to exercise self-control [1 Cor. 9:25]) for the prize. How well, however, Christians run to receive the prize (*brabeíon* [1017]) depends not only on themselves, but also on bystanders who may thrust themselves in the path of the race and become a stumbling block to the runners. The picture that the Apostle Paul wants to present to us as Christians is that we are to run the race with the consciousness that there is a prize to be won, and in order to win it we must struggle and exercise self-discipline. But it is also our passive duty not to be a stumbling block to others who are running.

"Continue to Become Inoffensive"

This verse begins with the adjective *apróskopoi*, from the privative *a* (1), not or without, and the noun *proskopé* (4349), the act

181

of stumbling, or *próskomma* (4348), that on which one stumbles, and from the verb *proskópto* (4350), to stumble, derived from *prós* (4314), to or against, and *kóptō* (2875), to cut, to strike. Paul's admonition is that we, as Christians, must not become something on which others can stumble.

The verb that is used is *gínesthe*, the second person plural present middle deponent imperative of *gínomai* (1096), to become. If this were an initial becoming, the aorist *genḗthēte* would have been utilized, but it is the present imperative tense that is used which would be more accurately translated as "continue to become." When a Christian begins to run the race himself, he then becomes conscious of the fact that at any time he may become a stumbling block to others who are also in the race with him. When the Apostle Paul was given permission by Felix, the Roman governor of Judea, to give an account of himself, he made an impressive statement: "And herein do I exercise myself [*askō* {778}, to exert all one's diligence, study, and industry, to endeavor, to strive, which is found only here] to have always a conscience void of offense [*apróskopon*] toward God and toward men" (Acts 24:16). The word *askéō* or the contracted *askō*, is a verb meaning exercise. The noun *áskēsis* is derived from this verb and is not found in the New Testament. That it means training in athletics is clearly indicated. The fact that it is a personal effort is indicated by the personal pronoun *autós* (846), I, myself, and it is an exercise which no one else can perform for another.

To have a conscience void of offense (*apróskopon*) takes conscious effort on the part of an individual. The Apostle Paul tried to develop this in himself, and he is advising the Corinthian Christians to individually develop the same in themselves. In Acts 24:16 what is translated "to have" is the present participial form of *échōn* which comes from the verb *échō* (2192), to have (MT), and *échein*, the present infinitive (TR). This indicates that the Apostle Paul was careful at all times not to be offensive to anyone. His tender conscience was directed "toward God and toward men." Notice that Paul "always" (*diá pantós* from *diá* [1223], through; and *pantós*, the genitive singular neuter of *pás* [3956], all) makes this his way of life at all times.

What is conscience? In Greek it is *suneídēsis*, which the Apostle Paul constantly mentions in this discussion (1 Cor. 8:7 [twice], 10, 12; 10:25, 27–29 [twice]). It is derived from the preposition *sún* (4862), together with, conjointly, and the verb *eídō* (1492), to perceive, to know intuitively. Therefore, conscience is something that one knows together with someone else. The "someone else" is God or the indwelling Holy Spirit (Rom. 9:1). In Acts 10:9–16; 11:4–14, as Peter was being prepared to introduce the gospel to the Gentile Cornelius and others, the Lord revealed to him through a dream that he was not allowed to classify anyone as clean or unclean. In fact, Peter was commanded to kill and eat any of the animals which he saw in the sheet lowered from heaven, although some were unclean (Acts 10:13, 14). Compare Leviticus 11 and Deuteronomy 14.

Additional Teaching on Individual Choices

The important thing is not what we eat, but how it affects other people. Our eternal salvation does not depend on our choice to do or not to do a certain thing. But of paramount importance is that we be *apróskopoi*, devoid of offense. We should take heed lest by a particular action we may offend a fellow believer. The privation of one's liberty should be preferred to becoming a stumbling block to another. Paul elaborates on this subject in Romans 14:14–23, which we shall do well to examine:

"I know, and am persuaded by the Lord Jesus, that there is nothing unclean of itself" (v. 14a). To put it in the context of 1 Corinthians 8—10, we could say that eating meats sacrificed to idols is not unclean in itself, but whether sin is involved depends on how it affects us or others who may observe us.

"But to him that esteems anything to be unclean, to him it is unclean. But if your brother is grieved with your meat, now you walk not charitably [or according to love]. Destroy not him with your meat, for whom Christ died" (vv. 14b, 15). We should be careful, then, as believers, not to offend others. The law of love should complement the law of freedom.

"Let not then your good be evil spoken of" (v. 16). We should beware lest that which we consider as right and beneficial be misinterpreted and become a stumbling block.

"For the kingdom of God is not meat and drink; but righteousness, and peace, and joy in the Holy Ghost" (v. 17). The kingdom of God is not merely rules and regulations, but spiritual achievements for which we must strive, even if that means material privation.

"For he that in these things serves Christ is acceptable to God, and approved of men" (v. 18). The word that is translated "acceptable" is *euárestos* (2101), well-pleasing, from the adjective *eu* (2095), well, and *aréskō* (700), to please. This is used in 1 Corinthians 10:33 in the phrase "even as I please all men." To be well-pleasing to God should be the foremost interest of every believer. The word translated "approved" in the phrase "and approved of men" is the adjective *dókimos* (1384), one who has been tested, from the verb *dokimázō* (1381), to find out whether one is truly pleasing to God.

"Let us therefore follow after the things which make for peace, and things wherewith one may edify another" (v. 19). Questions and statements that would bring divisions should be conscientiously avoided.

"Do not destroy the work of God for meat. All things indeed are pure; but it is evil for that man who eats with offense" (v. 20). In other words, Paul advises that divisions can come from such mundane things as food. Although food does not commend anybody to God, it sometimes destroys the work of God. The word translated "offense" in the phrase "for that man who eats with offense" is the word *próskomma* from which the word *apróskopoi*, devoid of offense, is derived. This same word *apróskopoi* is found in Acts 24:16. Maintaining the sacredness of the work of God is far more important than our right to eat or not eat.

"It is good neither to eat flesh, nor to drink wine, no, nor to do anything whereby your brother stumbles, or is offended, or is made weak." Here, in addition to eating meat, Paul also mentions "drinking wine." It is better to be an abstainer than to become a drunkard or to lead others into it, for there will be no drunkards (*méthusoi* [3183]) in the kingdom of God (1 Cor. 6:10). In our ministries around the world, we have experienced first hand the problems that can be caused in this very area. In one South American country where there is a great deal of poverty and fifty percent of the babies die before they are five years old, we have a large ministry to poor and needy children. A fine European Christian organization contributes heavily to this outreach and thousands of children are fed and clothed and won to the Lord. But the problem arises in that the European Christian community does not consider smoking or drinking to be wrong whereas the South American believers do. In such a case, the European leaders should confine their cigarettes and alcoholic beverages to their hotel room. Rather, they look upon the tender consciences of their South American brothers as foolishness, and thus they are offended. Paul tells us not to be offensive to anyone.

"Do you have faith? Have it to yourself before God" (Rom. 14:22a). Here again, as in verse 18, we have the matter of pleasing God as being predominantly important. Observe that in this verse Paul does not say "and approved of men," as in verse 18, or as would be more accurately translated, "and put to the test by men." Verse 22 declares that it is one's duty in such matters to have his own personal convictions of faith, which is here called *pístis* (4102), faith, persuasion, conviction. The word is "you" in the singular (*sú* [4771], the nominative singular second person personal pronoun). No group convictions enter here. Each one must resolve such matters before God and have his own personal convictions.

The next phrase, "have it to yourself," is *katá* (2596), according to; *seautón*, the accusative singular masculine third person form of the reflexive pronoun *seautoú* (4572), your own self. The Apostle declares that the conviction which you hold should not be something imposed by another person, group, or denomination, but is "according to yourself," a conviction that you came to personally. And then he says that this conviction must be made before God. The word "have" is *éche*, the second person singular present active imperative of *échō* (2192), to have. Notice that it is singular, "**thou** have it," no matter what others have.

The next statement, "Blessed is he that condemns not himself in that which he allows" (v. 22b), is the result of the first statement. What is the condition of the one who has personal convictions which are dictated by God rather than fellow-believers? This is expressed by the word *makários* which does not mean "happy," as is commonly mistaken, but "blessed," the word that we find in the Beatitudes in Matthew 5:11. Happiness refers to good fortune, well-being, and lightheartedness. *Makários* (3107) or blessed, means possessing the favor of God, that state of being marked by a fullness from God. It indicates the state of the believer in Christ (see the author's book on the Beatitudes, *The Pursuit of Happiness*). It also means fully satisfied. Who then is blessed? It is the one who is not condemned by what he tries or tests (*dokimázei*, the third person singular present indicative of *dokimázō*, to try, prove, discern, distinguish). The blessed person does not condemn himself in what he has tested and has found to be well-pleasing to God, and thus, has a personal conviction that it is right.

"But he who has doubts if he eats has already condemned himself that he has not *acted* out of faith, and everything that is not out of faith is sin" (a.t.). Whatever we do in this matter of eating, we must do out of the faith of God. If our faith demands that we should not eat, and yet we eat, we have sinned.

The third time that the word *apróskopoi* occurs is in Philippians 1:10: "That you may approve things that are excellent [*diaphéronta*, the accusative plural neuter present active participle of *diaphérō* {1308}, things different, the opposite of *adiáphora*, matters that make no difference as far as one's salvation is concerned, which is the word used to describe matters on which Christians have various views, nonessentials]; that you may be sincere and without offense [*apróskopoi*] unto the day of Christ." Paul's plea is that in things that make no difference in the Christian life, we should be devoid of offense. We should not busy ourselves so much with the nonessential things, such as whether we eat meats sacrificed unto idols, and neglect the things that are most important.

"Both to the Jews and to the Gentiles, and Also to the Church of God"

Paul mentions three groups of people for whom we must not provide any offense, consciously or unconsciously. Before each group there is the conjunction *kaí* (2532), "and." This applies to everyone, for the whole world can be divided into these three groups: the Jews, the Gentiles, and the church of God which is made up of people of both Jewish and Gentile backgrounds. Once individuals become members of the church of God, they cease to be what they were. They are God's own peculiar (private or special) people; no longer are they citizens of the world.

LESSONS:

1. Christians, by their behavior, can become stumbling blocks to other Christians in the race of life.
2. We must recognize what is offensive to others and try to avoid it.
3. We should take into consideration the cultural background of others who observe us.
4. "Nonessential" things really have no relationship to our salvation.
5. Christians are a group separate from all other groups of people in the world.

1 Cor. 10:33 | *Seeking the Advantage of Others Instead of Our Own*

> *In like manner, I accommodate myself to all people in all things, not seeking my own advantage, but that of many, so that they may be saved.*

Paul now affirms his message of verses 23 and 24 that he is determined to do not what he has the right to do, but rather that which is for the common good of the gospel and mankind. He will not do that which destroys, but that which builds up. He knows that people are different and that their differences need to be accommodated. The Jews ought to be treated as Jews, the Gentiles as Gentiles, and believers as believers. It was important that these groups recognize that Paul's contact with them was not selfish. In verses 25 to 31, Paul details examples of how to avoid selfish behavior.

"In Like Manner"

This verse begins with the adverb *kathṓs* (2531) derived from the preposition *katá* (2596), according to, and *hōs* (5613), as. Its literal translation is "even as" or "in like manner." The use of this phrase connects this verse with the previous one in which Paul's advice to the Corinthian believers was that they not become a stumbling block to all three classes of people among whom they lived, that is, the Jews, the Gentiles, and the Christians who make up the church of God. Paul wants his fellow Corinthian Christians to realize that he himself practices what he preaches, and there is not any group of people against whom he consciously discriminates. However, since his desire is for all to be saved, his concern is that he build societal contacts which hopefully will yield spiritual results, the salvation of those who are not saved and the edification of those who have been saved.

"I Accommodate Myself to All People in All Things"

To understand our verse, we must refer to what Paul is saying in 1 Corinthians 9:19–23. In verse 19, he declares himself to be free. Being freed by Christ, he has been delivered from the slavery of sin (Rom. 6:22). The verse says, "But now having been made free [*eleutherōthéntes*, the nominative plural masculine aorist passive participle of *eleuteróō* {1659}, to be free] from sin and become servants to God." Paul declares himself as having been freed from sin by Christ and having been enslaved to Him. "Having been enslaved" is *doulōthéntes*, the nominative plural masculine aorist passive participle of *doulóō* (1402), to enslave. Those who have been freed from sin and enslaved to Christ bear fruit unto holiness. In this state of holiness, Paul tried to be agreeable and pleasant so that he might win the most to Christ. The adjective *pánta*, the accusative plural neuter form of the adjective *pás* (3956), all, means in all things, but it does not mean in all things that the Christians want him to please them. It rather means that Paul does everything possible not to be obnoxious in order to accomplish his final desire which was, of course, to lead as many people as possible to Christ. The adjective *pásin*, the dative plural masculine adjectival form of *pás*, to all, has the meaning of indiscriminately.

The verb *aréskō* (700), to please, needs some clarification in this passage. The best contextual definition would be to accommodate oneself in attracting others to Christ in whatever manner holiness would permit. Paul is not trying to curry the affection of everybody he meets using any possible means. Nor is he trying to impress people to gain from them whatever he can. Three different portions of Scripture enable us to understand this verb *aréskō*. The first passage is found in Romans 15:1–3: "We then that are strong ought to bear the infirmities of the weak, and not to please [*aréskein*, the present infinitive of *aréskō*] ourselves. Let each one [*hékastos* {1538} which stresses the individual person in his behavior in developing a relationship with another] of us please [*areskétō*, the third person singular present active imperative of *aréskō*] his neighbor for his good [*agathón*, the accusative singular neuter form of the adjective *agathós* {18}, benevolent] to edification." The word "edification" is the translation of *oikodomḗn*, the accusative singular feminine form of the noun *oikodomḗ* (3619), edification, building up in process. And in verse 3, the verb *aréskō* occurs again, "For even Christ pleased [*ḗresen*, the third person singular aorist active indicative of *aréskō*] not Himself; but, as it is written, 'The reproaches of them that reproached Thee fell on Me.'" This passage teaches us that when the strong help the weak, they please Christ and help to win souls to Him; that each one of us will help to win our neighbor to Christ when we do acts of benevolence and help build them up; and that when we bear the reproaches of others, even as Christ did, we stand a very good chance of winning souls to Christ. The logical conclusion of this passage is that we should not try to be pleasant merely for our own benefit, but to win souls to Christ and bring glory to the name of our Lord.

The second passage is Galatians 1:10, "For do I now persuade men, or God? Or do I seek to please [*aréskein*, the present infinitive of *aréskō*] men? For if I yet pleased [*ḗreskon*, the first person singular imperfect active indicative of *aréskō*] men, I would not be the servant [*doúlos* {1401}, slave] of Christ." Paul says here that he is not merely trying to be popular and a man-pleaser, but that he is living in such a way that men, by observing his life, will be influenced to come to Christ.

The third Scripture is found in 1 Thessalonians 2:4: "But as we were allowed of God to be put in trust with the gospel, even so we speak; not as pleasing [*aréskontes*, the nominative plural masculine present active participle of *aréskō*] men, but God which tries our hearts." Now in reading 1 Corinthians 9:19–22, we see that the Apostle Paul means that within his Christian character, he must accommodate himself with respect to the cultural differences of diverse groups of people for the purpose of building relationships that will be instrumental in winning many to Christ.

"Not Seeking My Own Advantage, but That of Many"

This portion of verse 33 describes the manner of life Paul urges Christians to live. No matter to what group people belong, selfishness can be detected miles away. "Not seeking" is *mḗ* (3361), the relative "not"; *zētṓn*, the nominative singular masculine present active participle of *zētéō* (2212), to seek. The Apostle Paul recognizes the instinct of self-preservation. Love of self is natural, the product of our human nature. This is why our Lord, in confirming Leviticus 19:18, said, "You shall love your neighbor as yourself" (Matt. 19:19; 22:39; Mark 12:31; Luke 10:27). Paul even repeats that in Romans 13:9 and Galatians 5:14. See also James 2:8. But the teaching of Christ and Paul and James is that to love self, which is natural, should be supernaturally extended to others, since Christ died to reconcile us to God while we were still His enemies (Rom. 5:10). The thesis of the Apostle Paul in 1 Corinthians 8, 9, 10 is that we should consider others as much and even more than we consider ourselves. The Lord and the Apostle Paul do not want us to be negligent of ourselves, but they do not want us not to put ourselves on a throne and think of self constantly, which is expressed by the use of the present participial form of the verb. Also, the negative "not" is not absolute, but the relative *mḗ*.

The verbal noun which we translated "advantage" is *sumphéron*, the neuter present active participle of *sumphérō* (4851) used here as a verbal noun. It is derived from *sún* (4862), with, together, and the verb *phérō* (5342), to bring. Therefore, in this verse, *sumphéron* means to bring everything together for a self-serving advantage. The Apostle Paul then is not condemning self-preservation, but rather selfishness. A person who constantly seeks to take advantage of others is easily detected, and his usefulness in the kingdom of God is void. Such a person cannot even be a Christian, let alone lead others to Christ, which was the very purpose of the life of Paul. Paul's concern was for the many who needed him and whom he could serve only through his own self–denial and privation.

"So That They May Be Saved"

This last phrase summarizes the whole purpose of the life of Christ and that of Paul and all true followers of Jesus Christ.

"That they may [*hína* {2443}, for the purpose of] be saved [*sōthṓsi*, the third person plural aorist passive subjunctive of *sṓzō* (4982), to save]." The usage of the aorist tense indicates the initial salvation that joins people to Jesus Christ. Our goal and purpose in life is to bring the lost into the kingdom of God, and insofar as the church of God is concerned, its great need is the preservation of the unity of the spirit, which a selfless life such as Paul's would enhance greatly.

What a wonderful legacy is ours! What a goal to reach for! What a privilege to do all for the glory of God!

LESSONS:

1. Paul's desire was not to please men as in a popularity or political contest.
2. Having been enslaved by Jesus Christ, his one desire was that others might see Christ in him and be attracted to Him.
3. Although Jesus Christ and the Apostle Paul taught that the love of self is a natural instinct, it should be extended supernaturally to others.
4. One cannot win people to Jesus Christ by being self-centered and taking advantage of them.
5. The consuming desire of the Apostle Paul was to live for Christ and others. This is why his philosophy of life was summarized in Philippians 1:21: "To me to live is Christ and to die is gain."

Bibliography

Banks, Louis Albert. *The Great Promises of the Bible.* Eaton & Mains, 1906.

Blair, J. Allen. *Living Wisely.* Neptune, New Jersey: Loizeaux Brothers, 1973.

Locke, Rev. Clinton. "A New Year's Talk." In *The Churchman's Pulpit,* 2, (1910): 476, 477.

Hastings, James. *The Great Texts of the Bible.* London: Messers T. & T. Clark, The Waverly Book Co., Ltd., 1912.

Hastings, James, ed. *The Speaker's Bible: The First Epistle to the Corinthians.* Vol. 2, *The Epistle to Philemon.* 208–221. Grand Rapids, MI: Baker Book House, 1962.

Jones, J. D. *Elims of Life.* London: Religious Tract Society, 1911.

Jowett, Joseph. *Short Sermons.* London, Fleet Street: B. B. Seeley and W. Burnside, 1840.

Macartney, Clarence Edward. *Sermons from Life.* Nashville: Cokesbury Press, 1933.

Maclaren, Alexander. *St. Paul's Epistles to the Corinthians.* London: A. C. Armstrong and Son, 1910.

Matheson, George. *Moments on the Mount.* London: James Nisbet & Co., 1884.

Morgan, G. Campbell. *The Corinthian Letters of Paul.* London: Oliphants Ltd., 1954.

Morgan, G. Campbell. *The Westminister Pulpit,* Vol. 1. Fleming H. Revell Co., 1954.

Morris, Leon. *The First Epistle of Paul to the Corinthians.* London: The Tyndale Press, 1969.

Murray, Andrew. *The Power of the Blood of Jesus.* London: Marshall, Morgan & Scott, Ltd., 1947.

Redpath, Alan. *Blessings Out of the Buffetings.* Grand Rapids: Fleming H. Revell, 1993.

Simeon, Charles. *Expository Outlines—on the Whole Bible,* Vol. 6. Grand Rapids: Zondervan Publishing House, 1956.

Lexicons, Encyclopedias, and References for Greek Readers, from Classical and Koine Greek to Modern Greek

Byzantiou, S. D. *Lexikon tēs Hellēnikēs Glōssēs (Lexicon of the Hellenic Language)*. Athens: Koromēla, A., 1852.

Dēmētrakou, D. *Lexikon tēs Hellēnikēs Glōssēs (Lexicon of the Hellenic Language)*. Athens: Dēmētrakou, 1954.

Enkuklopaidikon Glōssologikon Lexikon (Encyclopedic Glossological Lexicon). Athens: Morfōtikē Hetaireia.

Enkuklopaidikon Lexikon Eleutheroudaki (Eleutheroudaki, Encyclopedic Lexicon). Athens: Eleutheroudakis, 1927.

Kalaraki, Michael and Nikolas Galanos. *Iōannou tou Chrusostomou Ta Hapanta (Complete Works of John Chrysostom)*, 1899.

Liddell, Henry George, and Robert Scott. *Greek–English Lexicon*, as Translated and Enriched by Xenophōn P. Moschos and Michael Kōnstantinides. Athens: John Sideris.

Megalē Helēnikē Enkuklopaideia (Great Hellenic Encyclopedia). Pursos (Pyrsos), Athens: Hēlios.

Neōteron Enkuklopaidikon Lexikon Hēliou (New Encyclopedic Lexicon "Hēlios"). Athens: Hēlios.

Papaoikonomou, George L. *Lexikon Anōmalōn Rhēmatōn (Lexicon of Irregular Verbs)*. Athens: Kagiaphas.

Stamatakou, J. D., *Lexikon Archaias Hellēnikēs Glōssēs (Lexicon of the Ancient Hellenic Language)*. Athens: Petrou Dēmētrakou, 1949.

Works by Spiros Zodhiates

Editor, *The Complete Word Study Dictionary: New Testament*. Chattanooga: AMG Publishers, 1992.

Was Christ God? Grand Rapids, Michigan: Wm. B. Eerdmans Publishing Co., 1970.

The Pursuit of Happiness. Chattanooga: AMG Publishers, 1987.

List of Abbreviations

acc. (accusative)

act. (active)

aor. (aorist [2 aor. for second aorist])

cf. (compare)

ch. (chapter)

comp. (composition)

dat. (dative)

etc. (and so forth)

ff. (following)

gen. (genitive)

i.e. (that is)

imperf. (imperfect)

indic. (indicative)

inf. (infinitive)

KJV (King James Version)

MT (Majority Text)

mid. (middle)

n. d. (no date available)

N. p. (no publisher available)

NASB (New American Standard Bible)

NIV (New International Version)

NKJV (New King James Version)

nom. (nominative)

p. (page), pp. (pages)

part. (participle, participial)

pass. (passive)

perf. (perfect)

pl. (plural)

pres. (present)

pron. (pronoun)

Sept. (Septuagint)

sing. (singular)

TR (Textus Receptus)

UBS (United Bible Society)

usu. (usually)

v. (verse), vv. (verses)

vol. (volume)

Guide to the Transliteration and Modern Pronunciation of the Greek Alphabet

Capital Letter	Small Letter	Greek Name	Trans-literation	Phonetic Sound	Example
A	α	alpha	*a*	a	as in father
B	β	bēta	b	v	as in victory
Γ	γ	gamma	*g*	y	as in yell (soft gutteral)
Δ	δ	delta	*d*	th	as in there
E	ε	epsilon	*e*	e	as in met
Z	ζ	zēta	*z*	z	as in zebra
H	η	ēta	*ē*	ee	as in see
Θ	θ	thēta	*th*	th	as in thin
I	ι	iōta	*i*	i	as in machine
K	κ	kappa	*k*	k	as in kill (soft accent)
Λ	λ	lambda	*l*	l	as in land
M	μ	mē	*m*	m	as in mother
N	ν	nē	*n*	n	as in now
Ξ	ξ	xi	*x*	x	as in wax
O	ο	omicron	*o*	o	as in obey
Π	π	pi	*p*	p	as in pet (soft accent)
P	ϱ	ro	*r*	r	as in courage
Σ	σ,ς*	sigma	*s*	s	as in sit
T	τ	tau	*t*	t	as in tell (soft accent)
Y	υ	ēpsilon	*u*	ee	as in see
Φ	φ	phi	*ph*	ph	as in graphic
X	χ	chi	*ch*	h	as in heel
Ψ	ψ	psi	*ps*	ps	as in ships
Ω	ω	omega	*ō*	o	as in obey

*At the end of words

SPECIAL RULES FOR THE TRANSLITERATION AND MODERN PRONUNCIATION OF THE GREEK LANGUAGE

COMBINATIONS OF CONSONANTS

Small Letter	Greek Names	Trans-literation	Phonetic Sound	Example
γγ	gamma + gamma	*gg*	g	as in go
γκ	gamma + kappa	*gk*	g	as in go
γχ	gamma + chi	*gch*	gh	as in ghost

DIPHTHONGS (DOUBLE VOWELS)

Small Letter	Greek Names	Trans-literation	Phonetic Sound	Example
αι	alpha + iōta	*ai*	ai	as in hair
αυ	alpha + ēpsilon	*au*	af, av	as in waft or lava
ει	epsilon + iōta	*ei*	ee	as in see
ευ	epsilon + ēpsilon	*eu*	ef, ev	as in effort or every
ηυ	ēta + ēpsilon	*ēu*	eef, eev	as in reef or sleeve
οι	omicron + iōta	*oi*	ee	as in see
ου	omicron + ēpsilon	*ou*	ou	as in group
υι	ēpsilon + iōta	*ui*	ee	as in see

BREATHINGS (Occur only with initial vowels)

(᾿)   Smooth, not transliterated or pronounced.
When words begin with vowels, it may occur at the beginning of words with every vowel or double vowel (diphthong). ἔργον—*érgon*, work; εὐχή—*euchē*, vow.

(῾)   Rough = h.
When words begin with vowels, it may occur at the beginning of words with every vowel or double vowel (diphthong). No distinction in pronunciation from the smooth breathing. To indicate the rough breathing we use "h" in the transliteration.

(ῥ)   Rho = r.

(ὑ)   Epsilon = u.
When these begin a word, they always have the rough breathing. There they are transliterated rh, hu, respectively. ῥέω—*rhéō*, flow; ὑπομονή—*hupomonē*, patience.

Scripture Index

DATE DUE   91